100

EASY
PERENNIALS

Natalia K. Hamill

PUBLICATIONS INTERNATIONAL, LTD.

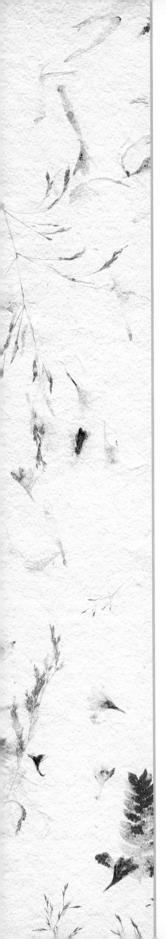

Natalia K. Hamill holds a bachelor's degree in horticulture and is the former horticulture editor of *Flower and Garden* magazine. She helped launch a retail garden center specializing in perennials and grows hundreds of perennials in her home garden. Natalia has contributed to a number of gardening books, including *The New Rose* and the *Complete Book of Gardening*. She also writes regularly about gardening for magazines such as *Gardening How-To*. She lectures and teaches classes about all aspects of perennial gardening and garden design.

Louis Weber, CEO
Publications International, Ltd.
7373 North Cicero Avenue
Lincolnwood, Illinois 60712

Manufactured in China.

8 7 6 5 4 3 2 1

ISBN: 0-7853-2971-4

Front cover: **Brian Warling Photography** (top left)

Back cover: **Jerry Pavia** (center)

Bill Beatty: 13, 40 (center), 180, 183, 186; **C. Colston Burrell:** 6-7, 12, 15, 38, 73 (top), 74 (center), 87, 95, 116, 124, 129, 135, 157, 168, 171, 184; **Derek Fell:** 40 (left), 43, 85, 88, 91, 96, 101, 102, 109, 112, 113, 122, 130, 131, 138, 142, 151, 153, 159, 161, 163, 165, 167, 175, 179, 181, 185; **Natalia Hamill:** 9 (bottom), 16, 24, 74 (right), 99, 128, 134, 137, 146; **David Liebman:** 10, 19, 21, 25, 60, 74 (left), 76 (top), 79 (bottom), 92, 108, 133, 136, 139, 141, 148; Wenner Liebman: 119: **Jerry Pavia:** 9 (top), 48, 72, 76 (bottom), 84, 89, 90, 93, 98, 98, 100, 103, 106, 107, 110, 111, 114, 115, 117, 118, 120, 121, 123, 125, 127, 132, 143, 145, 147, 149, 152, 155, 156, 158, 164, 166, 169, 172, 174, 182, 188; **Positive Images:** Patricia J. Bruno: 8, 17 (bottom), 18, 49 (bottom), 56 (bottom), 57; Karen Bussolini: 56 (top), 94; Les Campbell: 11 (bottom), 54; Harry Haralambou: 47, 62, 150; Margaret Hensel: Table of contents, 20, 23; Jerry Howard: 17 (top); Lee Lockwood: 176; Jacob Mosser III: 69; Ben Phillips: Table of contents, 41 (top), 49 (top), 58, 59 (top), 86, 104, 144, 154, 160, 162, 170, 173, 187; Pam Spaulding: Table of contents, 11 (top), 14, 22, 39, 40 (right), 41 (bottom), 44, 82-83, 105, 140; Albert Squillace: 53, 59 (bottom), 126, 177, 178.

Illustrations: **Mike Muir; Keith Ward.**

Map illustrations: **American Horticultural Society; Susan & Mark Carlson/Publisher's Art.**

CONTENTS

Chapter 3
DESIGNING WITH PERENNIALS
38

Improve your eye for choosing stunning perennial combinations after considering plant color, form, texture, and bloom sequence. Learn how to combine perennials with other plants, such as annuals, bulbs, and shrubs, to enhance your garden's overall effect.

Chapter 4
PLANTING AND CARING FOR PERENNIALS   48

Now it's time to get your garden growing! Gain insight into when and how to plant perennials—and what to do once they are in the ground. Prevent potential problems and learn how to attack those that may arise.

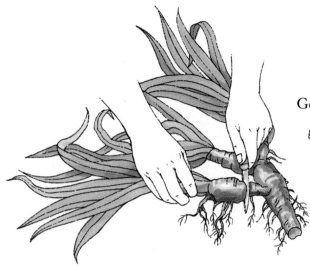

EASY PERENNIAL INFORMATION

Perennials are the ultimate garden plants. They come back, year after year, bringing cheer and beauty to your surroundings. And no matter where you live, growing and maintaining perennials can be easy if you have the knowledge you need to succeed.

Which perennials you end up planting will depend primarily on where you live. When you choose plants that are likely to survive—and thrive—in your area, working with perennials will be a joy. Such a variety of perennial plants exists that the choices are almost as wide as your imagination will allow.

Open yourself up to the endless possibilities you can explore as you turn the following pages to learn more about the wonderful world of perennials. You will learn how to plan, prepare, and plant a successful perennial garden. When you are done, you will have the newfound ability to create something unique that will bring you pleasure for years to come. So take some time to make your thumb a little greener and see what the world of perennials has in store!

White Coneflowers

Chapter 1
GETTING STARTED WITH PERENNIALS

WHAT ARE PERENNIALS? Perennials are a varied group of long-lived plants that provide years of color and gardening pleasure. One of the key differences between perennials (pronounced "pah-REN-ee-ahls") and annuals is that perennials survive winter outdoors, then produce new growth and flowers the following season. Annuals, on the other hand, germinate, grow, flower, produce seed, and die in a single season. Annuals must be planted every year while perennials are more or less permanent in the garden after they have been planted.

Another distinguishing characteristic of perennials is that most of them are herbaceous. Simply put, an herbaceous plant is a nonwoody plant that dies to the ground each year and reemerges the following season from growth points below the soil. Peonies, irises, and daylilies are well-known examples of herbaceous perennials. There are also a few evergreen perennials, such as Cheddar pinks (*Dianthus gratianopolitanus*), Japanese spurge (*Pachysandra terminalis*), and Lenten rose (*Helleborus orientalis*), that survive winter above ground with green leaves.

Peonies, foxgloves, and irises

Unlike annuals that flower continuously for several months, most perennials only bloom for a few weeks. However, if you plan your garden with careful attention to ease of care, bloom sequence, handsome foliage, and winter interest, you can enjoy a perennial garden that will be in bloom for many months. Perennial gardens are intriguing because they never stay quite the same. Daily walks through the garden are filled with surprises as new plants come into bloom in ever-changing colors.

You will find that your perennial garden changes from year to year, especially during the first few years of its existence. A newly planted perennial garden looks pretty spare compared to the exuberance of a mature, three- or four-year-old garden. And there is always the

Heartleaf bergenia

chance that you will add and subtract plants over the years or rearrange plants to emphasize particular color or texture combinations.

Both new and seasoned gardeners can be rewarded with dependable beauty and many enjoyable hours in the garden by selecting reliable, easy perennials and matching them to their proper growing conditions.

NOT ALL PERENNIALS ARE CREATED EQUAL

While most perennials share the common characteristic of persisting in the garden year after year, there is a great deal of variation among different species in terms of life span, flowering season, heat tolerance, winter hardiness, and ultimate size. One key to growing perennials successfully is knowing something about the individual characteristics of the plants you choose. If you know what to expect from a particular plant, then you are more likely to place it in the proper location

and give it the kind of care that encourages healthy, vigorous growth.

Longevity or life span is one characteristic that varies greatly among perennials. Some perennials, such as peonies (*Paeonia* spp.) and hosta (*Hosta* spp.), are very long-lived with plants easily living 20 years or more. Other long-lived perennials include astilbe (*Astilbe* spp.), moss phlox (*Phlox subulata*), ferns, heartleaf bergenia (*Bergenia cordifolia*), Lenten rose (*Helleborus orientalis*), different kinds of sedum, and Solomon's seal (*Polygonatum spp.*).

Some perennials, such as columbine (*Aquilegia* spp.) and Shasta daisy (*Leucanthemum* x *superbum*), are decidedly less permanent. In the case of columbine, the original plant (also called the mother plant), sets seed and then dies. Then new seedlings emerge and replace the original plant. However, the seedlings of hybrid plants seldom look like the parent plant; that's why the blue columbine you may have originally planted might come back in different colors, such as red or yellow. Many varieties of Shasta daisy bloom vigorously the first year, then become weak or

'Songbird' columbine

die out the following season. These plants are said to "bloom themselves to death." Once you understand this, it's easy to keep fresh daisies going year after year by dividing the original plant and replanting the new divisions every two years. (For more information on division, see page 74.)

Although they are usually sold as perennials, plants such as foxglove (*Digitalis purpurea*), hollyhock (*Alcea rosea*), and sweet william (*Dianthus barbatus*), are really better classified as biennials. Biennials are plants that complete their life cycle in two growing seasons. They generally produce leaves the first year but not flowers. In the second year, they flower, set seed, and die. Once again, if

Foxglove

you know which plants fit this growth pattern you will know how to keep these plants as permanent garden residents. Just let them set seed and allow new seedlings to take the place of the original plants.

Perennials also differ from one another in terms of how many times they bloom each growing season. Some plants are genetically programmed to bloom only once per season,

Yarrow

so no amount of coaxing will get them to bloom again. Some perennials that exhibit this trait are astilbe (*Astilbe* x *arendsii*), bear's breeches (*Acanthus spinosus*), blue starflower (*Amsonia tabernaemontana*), goat's beard (*Aruncus dioicus*), Joe Pye weed (*Eupatorium maculatum*), and peony (*Paeonia* hybrids). Because these plants bloom for a relatively short time, it is very important to consider foliage texture, color, and plant shape as you design your garden.

Repeat-blooming perennials, such as coreopsis (*Coreopsis* spp.), purple coneflower (*Echinacea purpurea*), pincushion flower (*Scabiosa columbaria*), Shasta daisy (*Leucanthemum* x *superbum*), tall phlox (*Phlox paniculata*), valerian (*Centranthus ruber*), and yarrow (*Achillea* spp.), can bloom for many weeks—and even months—if the old flowers are deadheaded. Deadheading refers to pruning faded flowers from a plant. (For more information on deadheading, see page 58.) When designing with long-blooming plants like these, you generally want to consider flower color and form over foliage.

There are a few spring-blooming perennials referred to as ephemerals. Ephemerals are perennials that go dormant after flowering and dispersing seed. Spring-blooming woodland wildflowers, such as Dutchman's breeches (*Dicentra cucullaria*), Virginia bluebells (*Mertensia virginica*), and wake robin (*Trillium* spp.), are all garden-worthy plants when used in a woodland garden for spring interest.

As lovely as perennial flowers are, it would be a mistake to place emphasis exclusively on flowers. There is much beauty in the

Wake robin

textures and subtle colors of foliage: spreading silver-gray mats of snow-in-summer (*Cerastium tomentosum*); bold hosta clumps in various shades of blue-green, green and white, and gold; fine-laced fern fronds; leathery peony leaves that form shrublike mounds—the list of attractive foliage goes on and on. To design an attractive perennial garden that looks good all season, you need to

be aware of foliage as well as flowers.

Various hostas provide foliage interest.

The "Encyclopedia of Easy Perennials," beginning on page 82, lists 100 of the easiest perennials to grow and describes each plant's life expectancy, blooming season and length of bloom, foliage, growing preferences, and other useful information. Once you are familiar with these aspects of the plants you are considering, you will be better able to decide which plants are right for your garden.

USING PERENNIALS IN THE GARDEN Perennials can be used in many different ways in the garden. Ornamental grasses and brightly blooming flowers, such as purple coneflower, black-eyed Susan, and goldenrod, can be grown in bold masses in what is now known as the "new American garden style." Perennials can be mixed with smaller trees, flowering shrubs, evergreens, vines, and bulbs in a layered garden. Perennials and annuals happily coexist in the abundance of loosely arranged cottage gardens. Perennials can also

Purple coneflowers and ornamental grass make a nice contrast.

cover the ground under a tree or hold a slope that is too steep to mow. They can be grown in containers and used to mark an entryway, to brighten an outdoor entertaining area, or to mask a bare spot in the garden. (For more on gardening in containers, see page 15.) For the most part, the varied uses for perennials are as wide as your imagination.

CUT FLOWERS Many perennials make excellent cut flowers. If you enjoy bringing fresh flowers indoors, but hesitate to cut them from your regular gardens, consider setting aside a cutting garden. Find a spot that receives at least a half a day of sun and that has reasonably good soil (see page 26 for information on garden preparation and soil amendments). You might want to locate your cut-flower garden in an out-

of-the-way spot where you won't notice the missing blooms. Feel free to use both annuals and perennials in your cut-flower garden.

Pick blooming flowers and remove any spent flower heads to prevent seed pods from forming—many plants stop flowering once seed pods develop. To keep bouquets fresh for as long as possible, cut flowers in the early morning hours when the stems are tight with water (also called turgid). Use sharp scissors and cut long stems. Take a bucket filled with warm water with you and immediately plunge fresh cut flower stems in water. When you bring the flowers indoors, strip all the leaves from the stems and place them in warm water with a bit of floral preservative. Change the water frequently and recut stems to keep flowers looking their best.

PERENNIALS FOR A CUT FLOWER GARDEN

Aster	Lupine
Black-eyed Susan	Peony
Blanket flower	Pincushion flower
Coreopsis	Poppy
Feverfew	Purple coneflower
Foxglove	Shasta daisy
Gayfeather	Siberian iris
Goldenrod	Sweet william
Heliopsis	Valerian
Hollyhock	Yarrow

Leaves are an important part of flower arrangements, too. Experiment with handsome foliage from the garden such as silvery artemisia, ferny astilbe, straplike daylily, lacy fern, bold hosta, and spiky Siberian iris leaves.

WILDLIFE If you enjoy the sight of various insects and birds frolicking in your garden, you're in luck. Many perennials are rich with the nectar that attracts butterflies and hummingbirds, and some form attractive seed heads that appeal to other birds. Planning and planting a wildlife garden is similar to planning and planting any other kind of garden—except you select plants based on the food and shelter they can provide.

Butterflies are cold-blooded, so their activity is limited to warm days. Since they will almost always be found feeding on plants in full sunlight, the first step is to locate a butterfly garden in a sunny area that is protected from the wind. Once you've selected a garden site, prepare the soil as you would for any garden. Plant generous quantities of host plants for young caterpillars (also called larvae) and nectar plants for adult butterflies. Host plants are those that are grown specifically to serve as egg-laying sites for female butterflies and food for caterpillars. Keep in mind that a caterpillar is a veritable eating

machine and the plants you provide for larvae will be almost entirely consumed. But providing host plants for the larval stage of the butterfly life cycle is just as important as providing nectar sources for adult butterflies.

You can use a combination of annuals, perennials, vines, and herbs in your butterfly garden. Herbs in the carrot family, such as parsley, dill, and fennel, are great host plants for swallowtail butterflies. Chives are an early

Monarch larvae feed on plants in the milkweed family.

blooming herb that provide much needed nectar for the first butterflies of the season. Annuals such as cosmos and zinnias are absolute butterfly magnets and will be covered with a variety of butterflies all season long.

In terms of perennials, plants in the milkweed family, such as orange butterfly weed (*Asclepias tuberosa*) and pink swamp milkweed (*A. incarnata*), are host and nectar plants for monarch butterflies. In fact, female monarchs only lay eggs on plants in the milkweed family, as it is the only group of plants young monarch caterpillars can feed on. Other good butterfly-attracting perennials include asters (*Aster* spp.), bee balm (*Monarda* spp.), butterfly bush (*Buddleia davidii*), catmint (*Nepeta* x *faassenii*), purple coneflower (*Echinacea purpurea*), gayfeather (*Liatris* spp.), goldenrod (*Solidago* spp.), lupines (*Lupinus* hybrids), garden phlox (*Phlox paniculata*), black-eyed Susan (*Rudbeckia* spp.), and tall stonecrop (*Sedum* x 'Autumn Joy').

If you find hummingbirds intriguing, try planting bleeding heart (*Dicentra spectabilis*), bee balm (*Monarda* spp.), cardinal flower (*Lobelia cardinalis*), catmint (*Nepeta* x *faassenii*), columbine (*Aquilegia* hybrids), coral bells (*Heuchera* hybrids), gayfeather (*Liatris* spp.), penstemons (*Penstemon* spp.), a variety of blooming sages (*Salvia* spp.), and sunset hyssop (*Agastache rupestris*). Vines and shrubs with

'Gateway' Joe Pye weed

trumpet-shaped flowers, such as honeysuckle (*Lonicera sempervirens*), trumpet creeper (*Campsis radicans*), and weigela (*Weigela florida*), are favorite nectar plants.

STOP AND SMELL THE FLOWERS

In addition to being beautiful and attracting wildlife, some perennials offer the added bonus of fragrance. Make sure you place these scented plants where people will be able to enjoy them, such as by a path, entryway, or bench.

Garden pinks
Hosta (especially *H. plantaginea*)
Lavender
Lily of the valley
Pink or white peonies (large-flowered)
Woodland phlox

Invite songbirds to your garden by incorporating perennials that form edible seed heads, such as asters (*Aster* spp.), black-eyed Susan (*Rudbeckia* spp.), Joe Pye weed (*Eupatorium maculatum*), willow leaf sunflower (*Helianthus salicifolius*), sunflower heliopsis (*Heliopsis helianthoides*), gayfeather (*Liatris* spp.), hosta (*Hosta* spp.), and purple coneflower (*Echinacea purpurea*). Shrubs and small trees that provide berries or shelter and water for drinking and bathing also aid in attracting songbirds. Flowering crabapples, dogwoods, hawthorns, deciduous and evergreen hollies, magnolias, mountain ash, pyracantha, serviceberry, and viburnums provide berries. Dense shrubs such as forsythia and lilacs, and evergreens such as evergreen hollies, junipers, pines, and spruces, provide year-round shelter for birds. If you plant a variety of desirable perennials, shrubs, and trees you should have great success attracting birds to your garden all year long.

GROWING PERENNIALS IN CONTAINERS In most instances, perennials are grown in the ground. However, there are many reasons that you might want to grow them as potted plants in decorative containers. Perennials offer a nice contrast to the annuals we usually see in pots. Container-grown perennials also offer you the chance to experiment with new plant combinations before placing them in the garden. Containers can be used singly or in groups and can be moved according to each gardener's need. Where garden space is limited—or nonexistent—such as on an apartment balcony, deck, or a patio, containers become a colorful focal

Fringed bleeding heart

point. They can also be used to emphasize an entryway or to disguise a bare spot in the garden. Another good reason to garden in containers is when you want to grow perennials that require special conditions, such as alpine plants that thrive in very sharply drained soil. Perennials that are of questionable cold hardiness are also good candidates for containers because they can be moved to a protected environment for the winter months.

Several perennials do well in containers. Fringed bleeding heart (*Dicentra eximia*) grows well in a container if placed in a shaded location and kept moist. Mat-forming bugle weed (*Ajuga reptans*), feltlike beach wormwood (*Artemisia stelleriana* 'Silver Brocade'), creeping thyme (*Thymus* spp.), and trailing sedums (*Sedum ellacombianum, S. sieboldii,* and *S. spathifolium*) make good, low-growing container plants. Threadleaf coreopsis (*Coreopsis verticillata* 'Moonbeam'), repeat-blooming daylilies such as *Hemerocallis* 'Stella d'Oro' and 'Happy Returns,' smaller hosta, coral bells (*Heuchera* hybrids), fragrant lavender (*Lavendula angustifolia*), and drought-tolerant purple sage (*Perovskia atriplicifolia*) are also excellent subjects for container plantings.

Select containers that mix well with the intended setting and that are in scale with the size of your plant or plants. Drainage is critical to growing healthy container plants, so be sure your container has adequate drainage holes in the bottom. If drainage holes are too small or are missing, make your own with an electric drill and a large bit. The choice of potting soil also affects how well moisture drains out of a container. Most perennials grow best in soil that is moisture retentive but well drained. Lightweight soil is best if you plan to move your pots around the garden. A commercial potting mix, containing sphagnum peat moss, vermiculite, perlite, composted bark, and a wetting agent, is ideal for most container-grown perennials. These mixes do not contain soil. If your potting mix does not contain fertilizer, you will need to add a slow-release fertilizer, possibly with a composition of 14-14-14. The numbers given to various fertilizer formulations represent the percentages of nitrogen, phosphorus, and potassium—N, P, and K—in the mix. A 14-14-14 formula contains 14 percent of each of these three elements.

If you grow more than one kind of perennial in the same pot, choose plants that like

'Happy Returns' daylilies

the same kind of growing environment. Don't try to grow shade-loving plants with plants that thrive in full sun, and avoid placing drought-tolerant plants with those that need a lot of moisture.

Container-grown plants require careful attention to watering and nutrition to look their best. When planting, be sure to leave about 3 inches between the top of the soil and the rim of the container so you have adequate space to water thoroughly. The soil moisture in containers should be checked daily during the growing season. Larger pots hold more moisture than smaller pots and do not dry out as quickly. When watering, fill the container completely to the rim, then allow the water to drain out. Refill the pot and allow it to drain again. This ensures that you soak the soil thoroughly and that water reaches plant roots. How often you have to water will depend on the moisture needs of the plants you are growing, the conditions they are growing in, and the time of year (make sure you check the "Encyclopedia of

'Burgundy Glow' bugleweed

Easy Perennials," starting on page 82, for the specific needs of each plant). Hot summer temperatures and drying winds cause plants to dry out quickly. For example, a container filled with moisture-loving ajuga and hosta will need more water than drought-tolerant purple sage (*Perovskia atriplicifolia*).

In addition to the slow-release fertilizer incorporated into your potting soil, you might also want to use a diluted liquid fertilizer during the summer to help keep plants blooming and growing actively. A blossom-booster formula, such as 10-30-20, can be used two or three times per month during the summer.

Most container-grown perennials require winter protection. All herbaceous perennials go through a dormant period triggered by short days and cool winter temperatures. The roots of garden-grown perennials are protected from freezing by the soil that surrounds them. The roots of container-grown perennials must also

be protected. A cool, unheated garage or shed is an ideal winter storage place. This environment will be cold enough to allow the plants to go dormant but not so cold that the roots freeze. Check pots with overwintering perennials every three weeks or so and water as needed so the soil doesn't go completely dry. Light is not a critical factor during winter storage but it is best to place pots where it is neither overly sunny nor completely dark.

As temperatures begin to warm and even out in the spring, begin watering the soil in your containers more often. Add a dilute solution of a balanced liquid fertilizer, such as 10-10-10 or 20-20-20. At the same time, begin adapting your container-grown plants to increased light and outside temperatures by setting containers outside in a lightly shaded, sheltered spot. Set plants out for a few hours at first, gradually increasing the amount of time they spend outdoors and the amount of sun they receive until they become acclimated. Add a light application of slow-release fertilizer—with a formulation such as 14-14-14—to the top of the soil after plants are fully acclimated

Asters

and in their outdoor homes. Apply a blossom-booster liquid fertilizer—with a formula such as 10-30-20—once per week throughout the growing season.

THREE TENETS OF EASY-CARE PERENNIAL GARDENING Growing beautiful, colorful perennials is an easy and enjoyable undertaking if you keep three simple tenets in mind.

1. Soil preparation is everything. Soil is the natural element most critical to gardening success. It supports and feeds plants and provides water and oxygen to roots. Loose, friable (crumbly) soil is a joy to work with. No amount of additional water, fertilizer, or plant coddling produces the same positive results as does thorough soil preparation. (See page 28 for detailed information on soil preparation.)

2. Put the right plant in the right place. As we said earlier in this chapter, not all perennials are created equal. Some perennials need at least seven hours of full sun to bloom while other perennials prefer after-

Coreopsis verticillata

noon shade. Still other plants need shade most of the day. Drought-tolerant perennials thrive in soil that dries out thoroughly while other perennials need a constant supply of moisture to their roots. Many of the native prairie plants we use in our gardens grow quite happily in average, clay-laden garden soil while woodland species need rich soil with plenty of organic matter. You can save yourself a lot of grief, money, and work by matching the right plant to the right growing environment. Make sure you take time to get to know the light, moisture, soil, and wind conditions in your garden.

Remember, too, that it's perfectly acceptable to move plants that aren't happy. If you find that some of your daylilies refuse to bloom because they receive too much shade, don't hesitate to dig them out and move them to a sunnier location. Likewise, if your Joe Pye weed grown in full sun wilts and turns crispy, move it to a spot with afternoon shade and moister soil. Read "Selecting a Garden Site" on page 22 to learn how to familiarize yourself with growing conditions in your garden.

3. "Low maintenance" is not the same as "no maintenance." Thoughtfully selected, easy-to-grow perennials planted in properly prepared soil should not require intense care after they are established. But there is a dif-

ference between moderate care and no care; you can't turn your back on a perennial garden for a month at a time and expect it to look good. Most perennial gardens require some weeding, watering, and plant grooming (removing brown foliage or spent flowers). If done once a week, these tasks are pleasurable and manageable. Take a look at "Grooming and Maintaining Perennials" on page 57 for tips that make caring for perennials easy.

EASY-CARE PERENNIAL QUALITIES Most of the improvements in modern perennials have come about due to the work of individual people involved in relatively small wholesale perennial growing operations or by keen gardeners with a discerning eye for superior plants. Large flower breeding companies are just beginning to concentrate on developing easy-to-grow perennials. The main reason for this is that most large seed companies are primarily interested in plants that can be grown from seed, like annuals and vegetables. Perennials, on the other hand, are generally vegetatively (also called asexually) propagated. That is, new plants are formed directly from mother plants by divisions, offsets, or cuttings. Companies that specialize in growing vegetatively propagated perennials are generally smaller and have fewer

resources than large bedding plant companies, so improvements to perennials have lagged a bit behind improvements to annuals. However, as perennial sales continue to increase, you can expect to see great advances in easy-care qualities over the next few years.

That said, there are a number of traits that currently distinguish easy-care perennials. For a perennial to perform well in the garden it must be resistant to diseases and tolerant of pests that commonly afflict plants in your region of the country. For example, powdery mildew is a fungal disease that attacks two garden

'Marshalls Delight' bee balm

favorites: bee balm (*Monarda* spp.) and garden phlox (*Phlox paniculata*). Both of these plants are hit hard during warm weather by this disfiguring disease, which coats plants with an ugly white pallor and causes leaves to drop. Fortunately, several highly mildew-resistant bee balm cultivars have been introduced in recent years including the deep red

Monarda didyma 'Jacob Cline,' the rich pink *M. didyma* 'Marshall's Delight,' and *Monarda fistulosa* 'Claire Grace' with lavender flowers. Mildew-resistant phlox varieties include the white-flowered and long-blooming *Phlox paniculata* 'David,' *P. paniculata* 'Eva Cullum'

with clear pink flowers and a maroon eye, and *P. paniculata* 'Franz Schubert' with long-blooming lilac flowers.

Another indicator of an easy-care perennial is heat and cold tolerance. If heat tolerance is an issue where you garden, look for perennials that thrive in warm climates, such as sunset hyssop (*Agastache rupestris*) and gray santolina (*Santolina*

Russell hybrid lupine

chamaecyparissus). If you live where summers are cool, look for perennials that enjoy those conditions, such as lupines (*Lupinus* hybrids) and monkshood (*Aconitum* spp.).

Perennials with self-supporting stems and flowers also help keep garden care easy. One perennial that is notorious for flopping (falling over) is the peony. Many gardeners avoid peonies because they've sadly seen

flower heads bend to the ground after a heavy rain. Fortunately you can still grow easy-care peonies by selecting varieties that don't flop because they have fewer flower petals, such as single, Japanese/anemone, and semi-double forms.

Repeat bloom is another valuable quality in easy-care perennials. After all, if a plant is occupying limited garden space, it's nice if it blooms for more than two weeks during the year. Many perennials will bloom for a minimum of four to six weeks if you deadhead them on a weekly basis. Good repeat bloomers are yarrow (*Achillea* spp.) and Shasta daisy (*Leucanthemum* x *superbum*).

And finally, look for perennials that have clean foliage through most of the growing season. The leaves of some perennials turn brown and dry up after they flower. A few plants that have good-looking leaves when they are not flowering include hosta (*Hosta* spp.), barrenwort (*Epimedium* spp.), the yellow-flowered blackberry lily (*Belamcanda flabellata* 'Hello Yellow'), and coralbells (*Heuchera* spp.).

Once you have a solid understanding of the general differences in perennials, how they can be used, and what to look for in easy-care plants, you can move on to planning a new garden or updating an existing garden, as we will do in the next chapter.

Chapter 2
GARDEN PLANNING

MOST PERENNIALS ARE LONG-LIVED plants that will bring years of pleasure if you take care to do a bit of planning and prepare the soil properly before planting. The planning stage is twofold. It consists of learning about the general climatic situation in your growing region, and of paying close attention to specific growing conditions that occur on your property. Once you've done this homework, then it's time to move on to soil preparation. Building good soil and taking care of it is the best way to ensure that you have a healthy, easy-to-maintain perennial garden for many years to come.

CLIMATE The United States features tremendous geographic and climatic diversity. Because of this fact, there is great variation in the kinds of perennials that grow in different parts of the country. The plants and planting style of a billowing cottage garden in Ohio are much different than a xeriscape (drought-tolerant) garden in Colorado or a lush woodland garden in the Pacific Northwest.

Climate is the overriding factor that determines which plants grow in various regions of the country. Climate can be defined as the collective state of the earth's atmosphere at a specific place over a long period of time. It includes factors such as annual precipitation, temperature highs and lows, relative humidity patterns, and the number of frost-free days that occur in the region. Since you can't do much to change your climate, it is best to plant the kinds of perennials that enjoy your particular climate and give them the growing conditions they prefer.

Two of the resources you can turn to for detailed local climate information are your county Cooperative Extension office and the

Mexican hat

United States Department of Agriculture (USDA).

SELECTING A GARDEN SITE Certainly, much of what goes into a lovely garden has to do with design—the area surrounding the garden, the colors you choose, how you arrange plants, and similar aesthetic elements. But if you think of perennial gardening as a 50/50 split between design and science, then it's easy to see why a good deal of attention should be given to the physical environment in which you garden. After all, a garden is only beautiful if the plants in it are healthy and vigorous.

Delphinium

SITE ANALYSIS The process of observing and evaluating potential growing areas is called site analysis. Existing plants, exposure, sunlight and shade, moisture, wind, slope, and soil type and drainage are factors that must be evaluated before a new garden site can be selected. The easiest way to do this is to go outside with a pad of paper and a pencil and to make notes as you analyze your possible garden locations.

First, jot down existing plants or groups of plants you either want to keep or eliminate. For example, you may decide to keep the stately Southern magnolia while the overgrown forsythia can go. Also note unattractive areas that might need to be screened, such as your neighbor's long-forgotten, rusted-out '52 car. Likewise, record ideas for areas that should be enlivened, such as an outdoor entertaining area.

Next, you will want to determine the amount of exposure your potential garden site gets. Exposure is the orientation of your property in relation to sun and wind—the direction your garden faces. Exposure affects soil and air temperature, soil moisture, and the amount of sunlight a garden receives. The soil in a south- or west-facing garden warms much faster in the spring, gets hotter in the summer, and retains less moisture than the soil in a north- or east-facing garden.

Full exposure refers to a garden site that does not face in any particular direction, so it gets sunlight equally from all directions all day long.

Then it is time to check how much sun and shade the area gets. Because the earth moves around the sun—and we are tilted on its axis—patterns of sunlight change throughout the day in all areas except those with full exposure. It's important to know what kind of shade your garden site receives because different perennials grow best in different degrees of shade.

To really understand the dynamics of sun and shade in your garden, you'll need to watch the sun's progression across your property at different times of the day, and if possible, at different times of the year. Check your site at one-hour intervals beginning at 9:00 A.M. and ending at 6:00 P.M. Notice how much sun key areas receive and for how long. Also record the type of shade—if any—you are getting. Use the following descriptions to help you categorize your shade types.

🌿 Filtered shade occurs when open tree branches allow patches of sunlight to

Filtered shade is natural in a woodland garden.

FLOWERING AND FOLIAGE PERENNIALS FOR SUN AND SHADE

FLOWERING PERENNIALS FOR SUN

Blackberry lily
Black-eyed Susan
Coreopsis
Creeping phlox
Daylily
Garden phlox
Gayfeather
Goldenrod
Peony
Purple coneflower
Sedum, 'Autumn Joy'
Yarrow

FLOWERING PERENNIALS FOR SHADE

Astilbe
Bleeding heart
Coralbells
Columbine
Foxglove
Fringed bleeding heart
Goat's beard
Heartleaf brunnera
Lady's mantle
Lenten rose
Lungwort
Toad lily
Woodland phlox

FOLIAGE PERENNIALS FOR SHADE

Barrenwort
Canadian ginger
Hosta
Ferns
Japanese spurge
Sedge
Variegated fragrant
    Solomon's seal

flicker across the ground. Filtered shade moves constantly as branches sway in the breeze and the sun moves across the sky. Filtered shade is also called intermittent, dappled, or open shade.

🌿 Light shade is the term used when the light is bright but there is little or no direct sunlight. If there is direct sun, it occurs early in the morning or late in the afternoon.

🌿 Part shade refers to an area that gets direct sun for half the day and shade for half the day (between 9:00 A.M. and 6:00 P.M.). A tall wall or other object, or trees some distance from the area usually cast this type of shade. Also, a garden on the east side of a house generally receives morning sun and afternoon shade while a garden on the west side is usu-

ally shaded in the morning and then blasted by afternoon sun. Part shade is also called semi-, medium-, or half-shade.

🌿 Full shade occurs in wooded areas that feature a mixture of tall and short trees that obstruct the sun for most of the day. It is also called deep shade.

🌿 Dense shade is dark shade that lasts all day. Dense shade is often referred to as heavy shade. Only a few plant species will survive in dense shade.

Next, you will want to determine the amount of moisture your area receives. Rain, snowfall, and groundwater are all sources of moisture. The amount of natural moisture your garden site receives depends on many factors, including slope, large trees, precipitation, temperature, physical barriers, and groundwater. A physical barrier, such as a wall or a dense canopy of shade trees, can prohibit moisture from reaching the ground, creating areas of dry shade. Large, shallow-rooted shade trees—such as maples—soak up vast amounts of water and nutrients so the soil underneath them is not likely to support

Ferns and astilbes accent each other well in a shade garden.

Perennials That Thrive in Difficult Places

Drought-tolerant Perennials

Blanket flower
Golden flax
Gray santolina
Hyssop
Jupiter's beard
Lamb's ear
Lavender
Mexican hat
Penstemon
Poppy mallow
Russian sage
Salvia
Snow daisy
Snow-in-summer
Soapwort
Speedwell
Thyme
Wormwood
Yarrow

Moisture-loving Perennials

Bee balm
Bergenia
Cardinal flower
Daylily
Ferns
Globeflower
Hardy hibiscus
Japanese iris
Joe Pye weed
Meadowsweet
Moneywort
Primrose
Rodgersia

to pay special attention to the wind. Sustained wind causes soil to dry out and increases the amount of water given off by leaves (this is called "transpiration"). Even if the soil stays moist, plant roots often cannot remove moisture from the soil fast enough to keep up with the loss of water from their leaves, so the whole plant shuts down and windburn and scorching occur.

If your proposed garden site is plagued by strong wind, you might consider planting or building a windbreak. A windbreak is a screen that breaks the force of the prevailing winds during a particular time of the year.

A living windbreak, composed of a single or double line of trees or large shrubs (or a combination of both), will provide shelter for plants. Another option would be to construct a sturdy fence with two-thirds solid material and one-third small holes. Both types of barriers will break up gusting wind and cut it significantly for a distance of twice the height of the windbreak. Windbreaks even do some good up to a distance of ten times the height of the barrier.

Large bushes can create a living windbreak.

many other plants. At the opposite extreme, the bottom of a slope often traps water, keeping it wetter than higher areas. Underground springs or other types of groundwater also contribute to moist soil.

Wind is another factor that affects your garden. If you live near the seashore or in an area of the country pounded by gusting winds—such as western Kansas—you need

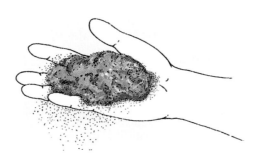

Sandy soil filters through your fingers.

As you analyze your property, keep in mind that growing conditions vary greatly from the top of a hill to the bottom. Hilltops are windier and drier than low areas. Low spots also trap cold air as it moves down slopes and settles in frost pockets.

SOIL The first thing you think of when considering a promising location for a garden is usually the soil. After climate, soil is the most influential naturally occurring condition that dictates what you can and can't grow. Soil is the garden's foundation, feeding and supporting the plants anchored in it.

Soil is composed of four main elements: mineral matter, water, air, and organic matter. Inorganic mineral matter originates from nonliving material, such as clay, silt, and sand. It composes approximately half of any given soil volume. But soil is also composed of organic matter (the decaying remains of once-living plants and animals), air, and water. Organic matter makes up about 1 to 5

percent of most soils, air takes up 25 percent, and water usually occupies another 25 percent of soil. All four of these elements are necessary to support plant growth.

Soils are classified by the size of the most prevalent mineral particle. Sand is the largest-sized particle. Sand particles are spherical in shape and do not fit together tightly. Sandy soil is like a box full of tennis balls—a lot of space and relatively little surface-to-surface contact. Sandy soil warms quickly in the spring, is light and easy to work, drains quickly, and is rich in oxygen. Plant roots and gardening tools penetrate sandy soil easily. However, this composition doesn't retain a lot of water or nutrients, so it dries out quickly and is lacking in plant nutrition. Unless they are well adapted, plants grown in sandy soil need frequent watering and fertilizing.

On the other hand, clay is a very small particle. There is very little space for air between these plate-shaped particles and

Clay-laden soil gathers into a tight ball.

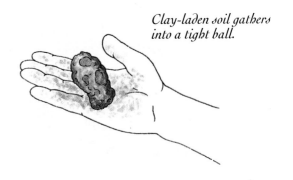

there is a lot of surface-to-surface contact. Clay soil retains moisture and nutrients longer than sandy soil but it is heavy and difficult to work, warms slowly in the spring, drains slowly, and contains little oxygen.

Silt is in the middle of sand and clay. Silt particle size and shape is between that of sand and clay. Therefore, it possesses some proper-ties of both of these materials.

Loam is a familiar term given to soil with a good balance of clay, sand, silt, and organic matter. Loam drains well, but doesn't rapidly become dry. It is rich in plant nutri-ents, has plenty of air space, and is easy to work.

To get a general idea about your soil type, gather a handful of moist soil and squeeze it. Clay soil forms a tight ball that doesn't come apart when you tap it. Sandy soil doesn't form a ball and runs through your fingers easily. Loam holds together when you squeeze it but falls apart when you tap it.

SOIL TESTING In order to get detailed, pre-cise information about your soil, you should have it tested by a laboratory. In some states,

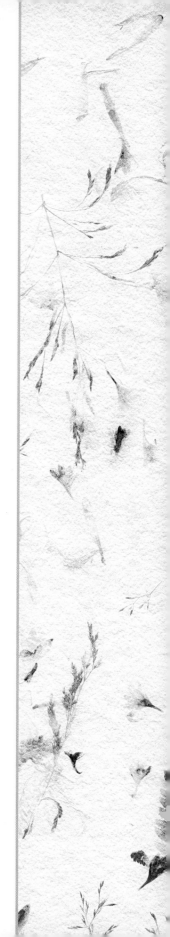

Loam is ideal garden soil.

the county Cooperative Extension office will do soil tests; in others, it's necessary to use the services of a private testing lab, which can be recommended by the local Cooperative Extension office. Soil testing facilities will send you a test kit consisting of instructions, an information sheet, a packet for your soil sample, and an address to mail the kit and payment to when they are ready.

Soil may vary here and there in your yard, especially if you've already done some soil amending or if builders brought in new topsoil before planting the lawn. Therefore, take several soil samples from different areas of your pro-posed garden site to get a good overview of your conditions. When the soil is dry, dig down 6 to 12 inches deep to get soil from the prime root zone. Take a tablespoonful from each end of the proposed bed and from the middle. Mix all the samples together thor-oughly in a single container to make a soil composite that will be representative of your entire garden area. Then mail the mixture to the soil lab.

Ask the lab for a complete soil test, including organic matter content. This might

cost you a little more, but you need to know how much organic matter is present so you know how much you need to add. Your test results will tell you what kind of soil you have, its pH (the acidity or alkalinity of your soil), and nutrient levels. The lab should also suggest some possible materials to add to your soil in order to improve it.

SOIL DRAINAGE The movement of water through soil is called drainage. When water moves quickly through the soil, drainage is considered good or fast. Such soil is referred to as well drained. When water moves slowly and stands on the surface, drainage is slow and the soil is poorly drained. Poorly drained soil stays cold and wet in the spring and doesn't allow seeds to germinate properly. Plants drown due to lack of oxygen in the soil and develop shallow roots. Roots and crowns (the location on a plant where the stem meets the roots, usually found at soil level) rot during the winter causing plants to die.

GROUNDWORK Once you've completed your site analysis and received the results of your soil test, you're ready to get the soil in shape for planting. Keep in mind that perennials will be residents in your garden for many years, so proper soil preparation is vital to

getting your plants off to a good start. Paying special attention to this phase of garden preparation will reward you in the long run with perennials that easily double—and may even triple—their size in the first growing season.

If you are putting in a ground-level bed or a raised bed in an area that was previously devoted to lawn, you'll need to get rid of the grass first. Lay out the shape of your new bed with a watering hose or an orange indoor-outdoor extension cord. Use a sharp, flat-edged spade to cut vertically into the sod along the outline of your bed. Then, cut the sod into one-foot-square sections. Slide your spade under each section to sever grass roots and remove it. Shake off any excess soil before putting the sod chunks in a wheel-barrow or cart. Use these grass

Save as much of the existing soil as you can when preparing a new garden bed.

Using a rototiller can make short work of soil preparation.

pieces to patch bare spots in your yard or add them to your compost pile.

Next, loosen the bare soil with a spading fork or rototiller. Break up clods of dirt and remove stones. Also, be sure to take out as many of the remaining roots as you can. These are probably roots of perennial weeds. The more you can remove now, the less trouble you will have with weeds later.

Now is the time to add organic matter and any soil amendments. Organic matter is the most common and effective ingredient used to improve soil. Organic matter is decomposed plant and animal material that turns into humus. Humus is the sticky substance that is produced as living material decays. It improves soil structure by making particles

clump together in loose clusters instead of in heavy sheets of clay or transient rivers of sand. Soil that crumbles easily is said to be friable. Loose, friable soil is a joy to dig in. Organic matter also feeds plants and the microorganisms that live in the soil when it breaks down into life-giving nutrients. In general, organic matter is great stuff and your garden can never get enough of it.

Good garden soil should have at least 5 percent organic matter, which might be present in a woodland soil but is usually lacking in ordinary lawns. Spread organic matter 2 to 6 inches deep across your entire bed. The amount you add will be determined by the results of your soil test report and by the kind of plants you want to grow. Moisture-loving woodland plants need more organic matter than stalwart prairie natives. Organic matter can be added in the form of homemade compost, purchased compost, well-rotted manure, or leaf mold. Many municipalities have composting programs and offer compost free to residents if you have the means to haul it. As a rule of thumb, one cubic yard of organic material will cover 100 square feet to a depth of 3 inches.

If your soil test indicates that your soil pH is too high or too low, add lime or sulphur to correct it. A pH below 6.0 indicates the soil is on the acidic side and may need to be adjusted with dolomitic limestone. If the reading is over 7.2, the soil is too alkaline. To solve this problem, add powdered soil sulphur, or, for quicker results, iron sulfate. Any needed materials should be available at a full-service garden center. Be sure to carefully follow all soil-additive instructions.

Plant nutrients should also be considered at this time. As mentioned on page 16, fertilizer is commonly composed of some combination of the three major plant nutrients: nitrogen, phosphorus, and potassium—usually listed by their corresponding elemental symbols N, P, and K. Nitrogen produces vigorous, green leafy growth. It moves through soil easily so it can be applied at the surface of the soil and will move down to plant roots. Because of its mobility, nitrogen also leaches quickly from the soil during heavy rains and watering. Unlike other plant nutrients, nitrogen is not a soil mineral. It must come from decomposing organic matter, air, water, or inorganic fertilizers.

Add needed nutrients to the soil.

Potassium promotes root formation and gives seedlings a rapid start. Potassium does not move through the soil readily, so it needs to be incorporated at root level prior to planting.

Phosphorus is closely linked to nitrogen as it aids in photosynthesis. It helps fruit ripen and is important for the development of plump, full seeds. It also hastens blooming and maturity. Additionally, it improves disease resistance, stress tolerance, and general plant health. Like potassium, phosphorus should be added to the soil at root level because it does not move through the soil.

If the results of your soil test indicate a lack of certain nutrients, you should follow the recommendations for supplementing the soil. If the imbalance is slight, you can use organic fertilizers, which generally contain a low percentage of nutrients that are slowly released into the soil. Their gradual and often long-lasting effects may not be fast acting or concentrated enough for immediate results. However, to avoid using too much inorganic fertilizer, a compromise can be reached. Use the quick-to-feed commercial inorganic plant foods first (in limited quantities), and then follow up in subsequent years with natural, slowly released organic fertilizers.

If your garden soil is lacking in only one element, you can correct the deficiency with a fertilizer containing a single nutrient. Both organic and inorganic fertilizers are available as a single element or as "complete" fertilizers containing nitrogen, phosphorus, and potassium. Consult with your local Cooperative Extension office or another qualified horticulturist at a botanical garden, arboretum, or full-service garden center if you feel uncertain about solving nutrient deficiency problems.

Once all the organic matter and soil amendments have been spread across the top

ORGANIC AND INORGANIC FERTILIZERS

Plant nutrients can be supplied by organic or inorganic sources. Organic fertilizers come from the decaying remains of once-living plants and animals. As the organic residue decays, it releases valuable plant nutrients. Inorganic fertilizers are synthesized from coal or natural gas, or are made by treating rock minerals with acid to make them more soluble.

Plants don't recognize the difference between inorganic and organic fertilizers, so why should you care what you use? There are some notable differences between these types of fertilizers.

Soluble chemical fertilizers quickly feed plants but they do not provide improved long-term living conditions for beneficial soil microorganisms or help build good soil structure.

INORGANIC FERTILIZER

Pros
- Is readily available for plant uptake
- Can be used in small quantities
- Works quickly

Cons
- Can burn plants
- Repels beneficial earthworms
- Does not improve soil structure
- Does not feed beneficial soil microorganisms
- Can taint groundwater sources
- Must be purchased

ORGANIC FERTILIZER

Pros
- Can be obtained free of charge
- Will not burn plants
- Improves soil structure
- Feeds beneficial soil microorganisms
- Is natural and environmentally friendly

Cons
- Nutrients are released slowly; soil must be warm and microbes active for nutrients to be released
- Relatively large quantities are needed

Cultivate the soil to help get rid of weeds.

of the bed, mix them into the top eight inches of soil with a spading fork, shovel, or tiller. Use a rigid steel, bowhead rake to smooth the surface of the bed.

After amending your soil, run a percolation test to evaluate soil drainage. Dig a hole 12 inches across and 12 inches deep. Fill the hole with water and let it drain completely. Fill the hole again. This water should drain in less than one hour. If it doesn't, you'll need to add more organic matter or install drain tiles to improve drainage. Drain tile is a perforated plastic pipe that is laid below a poorly drained area. It captures excess water that would otherwise rot roots, and redirects it to an outlet area below the garden.

If possible, allow the soil to stand unplanted for several weeks after you finish working with it. Stir the soil on top (an inch or two below the surface) every three to four days with a shovel or hoe (called "cultivating") to get rid of fast-germinating weeds. Taking the time to perform this step will reduce your weeding chores during the rest of the gardening season.

The final step in preparing a garden bed is to install some kind of mowing strip or edging to keep grass and garden separate. Patio squares or slate pieces laid end-to-end at ground level work well. Other options include landscape logs, poured concrete strips, or brick pavers laid side-by-side on a sand or concrete base. A mowing strip must be deep enough and wide enough so grass roots cannot tunnel underneath or travel across the top to reach the flower bed. To save yourself tedious grass trimming, make the top of the strip low enough so that the wheels of your lawn mower can travel safely over the surface of the mowing strip.

MAKING YOUR OWN COMPOST Composting yard debris is becoming more popular as yard waste is systematically banned from landfills and the value of organic matter in the garden is better understood. Most homeowners can find an out-of-the-way place to recycle leaves and lawn clippings into compost. Here are a few easy composting options that might work for you.

♨ Till autumn leaves into the garden in fall to boost the organic content by spring

♨ Make a cold compost pile by heaping up vegetable leftovers and yard waste in a pile—or contain waste in a neat cubicle made of concrete blocks or recycled wood pallets

♨ Invest in compost-making equipment— bins, barrels, and buckets—specifically designed to make composting efficient

For the best results, try to keep a 2:1 ratio of brown material (rich in carbon) to green material (rich in nitrogen). Brown, carbon-rich material includes fallen leaves, chopped twigs, straw, strips of newspaper, and saw-dust. Green, nitrogen-rich mate-rial includes grass clippings, animal manure (not from a dog or cat), green weeds, flowers and foliage, and organic kitchen waste. Do not try to compost meat, fat, or any meat by-products (grease, drip-pings, etc.), as these

will attract animals and develop a foul odor as they decay. In addition to green and brown material, add some garden soil to introduce beneficial microorganisms and a bit of high nitrogen fertilizer to get the pile simmering. Keep the mix moist to promote insect, earth-worm, and fungi activity. Finished compost has an earthy smell and is dark and crumbly.

ORGANIC MULCH Biodegradable mulch, such as shredded leaves, shredded bark, cocoa bean hulls, and compost, when spread 2 inches deep, is a great way to smother weeds and to feed garden plants. As the mulch decomposes, it adds nutrients to the soil and improves soil structure just like other organic materials. One word of caution: Fresh grass clippings can rob garden plants of nitrogen and they tend to exclude air and water by matting down. Let grass clip-pings turn brown to remedy the nitrogen problem and mix with shredded leaves to prevent them from matting.
Read more about mulching in Chapter 4 on pages 52–53.

Composting saves money and helps the environment.

USDA PLANT HARDINESS ZONE MAP

One of the key pieces of climatic information you should become familiar with is the USDA Plant Hardiness Zone Map. This is a well-established system that uses the average annual minimum temperature to assign plant hardiness zone ratings to various areas of the United States. It divides the country into 11 zones with Zone 1 being the coldest and Zone 11 being the warmest.

Plants are assigned corresponding hardiness zone ratings based on the lowest temperature they will survive. Plant labels, catalogs, and reference books usually tell you a particular plant's USDA hardiness zone rating.

The Zone Map should be used as a general guideline for plant selection. Plants recommended for one zone might do well in the southern part of the adjoining colder zone, as well as in the neighboring warmer zone. Factors such as altitude, exposure to wind, and the amount of available sunlight also contribute to a plant's cold hardiness. The Plant Hardiness Zone Map is the single most useful guide for determining which plants are likely to survive in your garden.

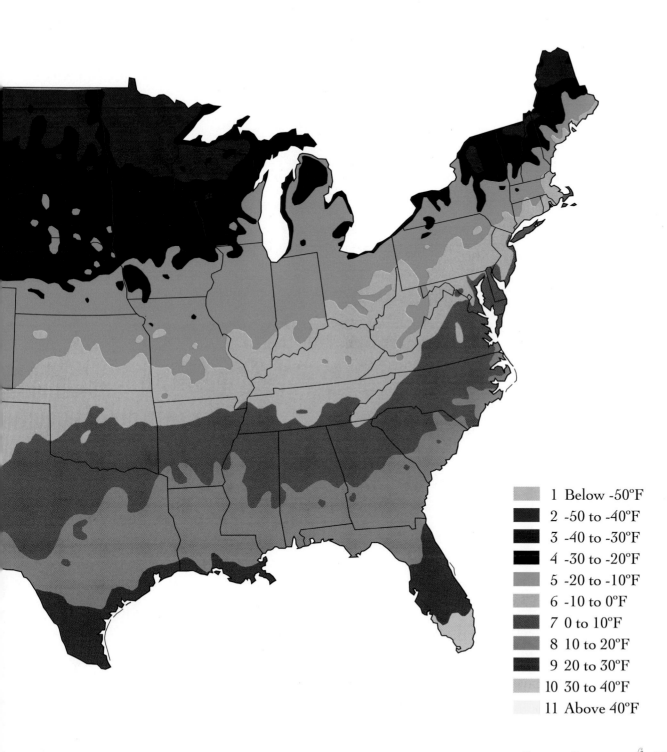

1 Below -50°F
2 -50 to -40°F
3 -40 to -30°F
4 -30 to -20°F
5 -20 to -10°F
6 -10 to 0°F
7 0 to 10°F
8 10 to 20°F
9 20 to 30°F
10 30 to 40°F
11 Above 40°F

AHS Plant Heat-Zone Map

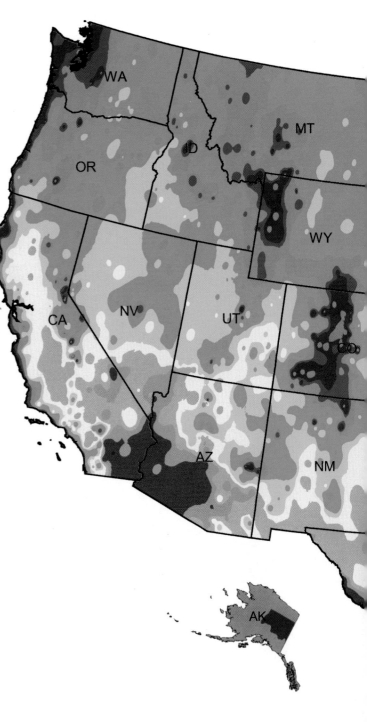

Selecting perennials based on their ability to handle summer heat is just as important as selecting them based on their cold tolerance. Extreme cold kills a plant that isn't hardy almost immediately, while perennials that aren't suited to prolonged heat languish and die over time.

Heat damage is most severe when the air temperature is high for several days in a row and, at the same time, soil moisture is in short supply. Signs of heat stress include wilted or brown leaves; chlorotic (yellowish) leaves; fewer, smaller blooms; and stunted growth. You can avoid this slow, painful death by selecting perennials that are adapted to your summer temperatures.

To help determine a plant's adaptability to heat, the American Horticultural Society (AHS) recently developed the Plant Heat-Zone Map. It divides the country into 12 zones based on the number of days when temperatures typically rise above 86°F. This is the temperature at which many plants suffer heat damage. Zone 1 has the lowest average number of days above 86°F and Zone 12 has the most days.

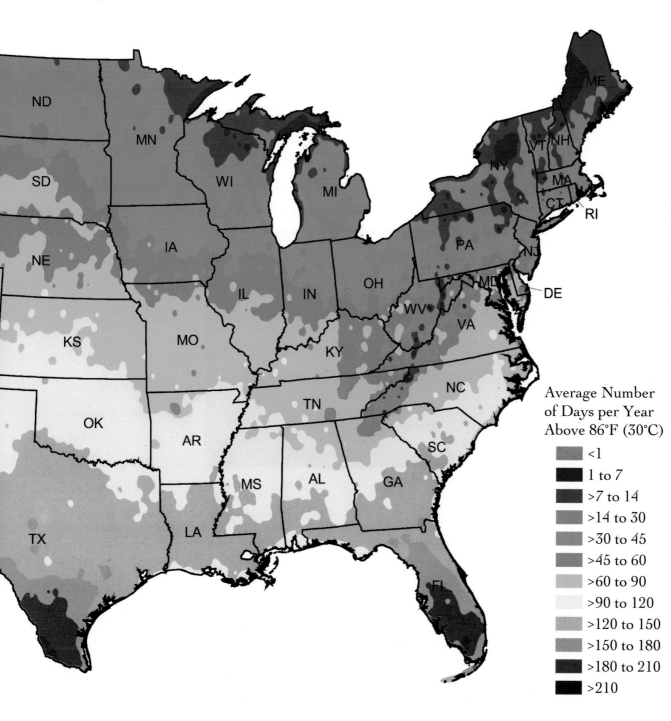

Average Number
of Days per Year
Above 86°F (30°C)

- <1
- 1 to 7
- >7 to 14
- >14 to 30
- >30 to 45
- >45 to 60
- >60 to 90
- >90 to 120
- >120 to 150
- >150 to 180
- >180 to 210
- >210

Chapter 3
DESIGNING WITH PERENNIALS

PLETHORA OF PERENNIAL POSSIBILI-
TIES AWAITS. No matter where you live
or what kind of conditions you garden in,
there are hundreds of perennials to choose
from. They come in every conceivable color
and size. The trick is figuring out which ones
you want to use and how you want to lay them
out in your garden.

Unlike an annual
garden that can sport a
new design or color
combination every year,
perennial gardens aren't
meant to change drasti-
cally from year to year.
And while almost any
combination of healthy
flowers is bound to be
pretty, chances are that you will be more
pleased with the results if you spend some time
thinking about the design you wish to use.

In addition to specific design elements
such as color, form, texture, season, and
length of bloom, you'll want to consider the
kind of growing conditions various plants
prefer and arrange them accordingly. It's

'Sea Shell' peonies

much easier to take care of a garden when
plants with similar cultural requirements—the
technical term for growth needs—are grouped
together. For instance, you wouldn't want to
plant different perennials that have both high
and low watering needs in the same area.

A good way to keep all this information
straight is to begin by
listing your favorite
plants on paper first,
noting their available
colors and cultural
requirements. It helps
to make columns of
information such as
height in inches, foliage
color, flower color,
season of bloom, sun or
shade, rich or light soil, and water requirements. Then you can scan down the column
and immediately see which plants are cultur-
ally compatible and how plants might interact
if you grouped them together in the garden.

A very easy approach to arranging plants
is to plan to put shorter plants toward the
front of the garden and taller plants at the

Fall-blooming false sunflowers and montbretia

back. As you narrow down the plants that work well together, you can actually see a workable garden emerge before your eyes. Don't worry too much about making a mistake—most perennials can easily be moved from one place to another if you discover that something isn't working out quite right.

COLOR The first thing that many people think about relative to garden design is color. The primary source of color is from flowers. But another equally important consideration is the color provided by existing backgrounds: fences, house walls, flowering shrubs, or the blossoms in neighboring gardens. If, for example, the background is painted white, white flowers planted next to it will become virtually invisible. If the area is backed by dark woods or evergreens, you should keep in mind that dark shades of blue and purple will disappear. Conversely, white, yellow,

silver-gray, and yellow-green perennials will stand out.

In addition to such physical considerations, there are also emotional ones. Color can set the mood of your garden. Red, yellow, and orange shades are bright, warm, and cheering. On the other hand, blues, silvers, and whites, are calming and cooling. These colors can be very soothing during the heat of summer. A nostalgic, romantic atmosphere can be established by using pale pastels. Also,

PERENNIALS WITH INTERESTING FOLIAGE COLOR

Yellow archangel
Cheddar pinks
Coral bells
Variegated ornamental grasses
Variegated, chartreuse, and glaucous
  hosta
Variegated Japanese iris
Variegated Japanese sedge
Lady's mantle
Lamb's ear
Lungwort/Bethlehem sage
Moneywort
Sedum
Variegated Solomon's seal
Spotted nettle
Wormwood
Silver-leaved yarrow

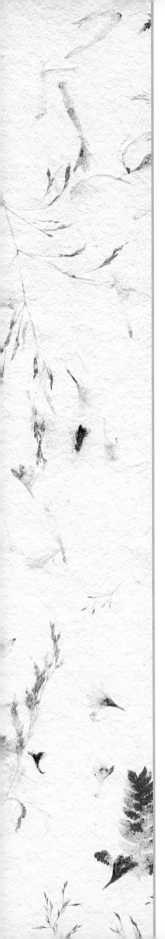

SELECTING PERENNIALS BY COLOR

One good way to start color planning is by listing some of the perennials that flower in the color range you are looking for. This is by no means a complete list (a lot of these perennials come in many colors), but it should give you an idea of how to begin.

WHITE

Astilbe
Baby's breath
Bleeding heart
Boltonia
Gaura
Goat's beard
Japanese anemone
Obedient plant
Tall phlox
Shasta daisy

BLUE

Aster
Bellflower
Blue mist spirea
Heartleaf brunnera
Catmint
Delphinium

Flax
Ladybells
Leadwort
Russian sage
Virginia bluebells

PURPLE

Aster
Butterfly bush
Purple coneflower
Gayfeather
Lavender

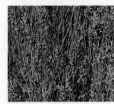

Salvia
Siberian iris
Garden phlox
Verbena

RED

Bee balm
Cardinal flower
Daylily
Hardy hibiscus
Peony
Maiden Pinks
Salvia
Yarrow

PINK

Astilbe
Bee balm
Bleeding heart

Chrysanthemum
Daylily
Garden phlox
Hardy hibiscus
Joe Pye weed
Peony
Garden phlox
Valerian
Yarrow

YELLOW

Blackberry lily
Black-eyed Susan
Yellow coneflower
Coreopsis
Daylily

Golden lace
Goldenrod
Peony
Yarrow

ORANGE

Blanket flower
Butterfly weed
Daylily
Hyssop

a vibrant, upbeat feeling develops when pure, bright colors are mixed. Think about the mood and atmosphere you'd like to create in each area of your garden; it may differ from one area of your garden to another, especially if you have a large property.

If you feel uncertain about color, you may want to use proven combinations with the help of a color wheel. There are three basic winning combinations. The first is monochromatic—it combines all of the various shades, tints, and tones of a single color. The second is complementary, and includes all of the variations of two colors exactly opposite each other on the color wheel. The last is analogous—those variations of three colors that are found adjacent to one another on the color wheel. These are not the only possible combinations, but they are the easiest and

Well-planned color and height make this border a lovely sight.

most certain to succeed.

Coralbells provide bold foliage color.

After considering flower and background colors you should also remember to think about foliage color. Many perennials only bloom for a short time during the growing season, so their foliage will be quite noticeable. Look for plants with variegated (striped, spotted, or marked with colors other than green), glaucous blue-green, maroon, chartreuse, or silvery-gray foliage.

Just two final hints on color: white flowers and silver foliage will blend easily with any other colors you select, and varying the intensity of different flower colors in your design will often help add vitality and interest to the planting.

SEASON AND LENGTH OF BLOOM

As you consider color, you'll also want to take into account when your perennials bloom and for how long. You don't want to inadvertently end up with a garden that is glorious in May but completely without color in

July. Similarly, it would be disappointing to find that the goldenrod and iris you so carefully placed next to each other don't bloom at the same time.

If you know the flower color, when it blooms, and for how long, you should be able to group plants with flowers that bloom at the same time in beautiful combinations. For instance, if you are looking for plants to use in a complementary color scheme of yellow and purple, yellow-flowered yarrow (*Achillea* 'Moonshine' or 'Coronation Gold') and purple sage (*Salvia* x *sylvestris*) are a classic combination that bloom together for all three of the summer months.

However, remember that beginning and ending bloom dates vary somewhat across the country. Northern gardeners will see plants

BLOOM SEQUENCE

This list should give you an idea of when selected easy-to-grow perennials begin blooming. If the plant has an asterisk (*) next to it, it blooms for more than 10 weeks if given the proper cultural care.

SPRING

Barrenwort
Bergenia
Old-fashioned bleeding
   heart
Blue star flower
Heart-leaf brunnera
Columbine
Bearded iris
Siberian iris
Lady's mantle
Lenten rose
Lungwort/Bethlehem sage
Lupine
Peony
Creeping phlox
Woodland phlox
Cheddar pink
Variegated Solomon's seal

SUMMER

*Black-eyed Susan
*Fringed bleeding heart
*Catmint
*Purple coneflower
*Threadleaf coreopsis
Daylily
Foxglove
Goldenrod
Hardy geranium
*Hollyhock
Hosta
Hyssop
Joe Pye weed
Maiden pink
Meadow rue
Penstemon
*Tall phlox
*Rose mallow

*Russian sage
*Salvia
*Sedum 'Autumn Joy'
*Shasta daisy
*Stoke's aster
*Verbena
*Veronica
*Valerian
*Yarrow

FALL

*Aster
*Boltonia
Japanese anenome
Leadwort
Hardy mums
Ornamental grasses
Toad lily

coming into and out of bloom approximately 10 to 21 days later than southern gardeners. The best way to track bloom sequence and duration is to keep a journal or make notes on a calendar of when various plants bloom in your garden and in gardens you visit. It also helps to take pictures and date them on the back. This will also aid you in finding new plant combinations.

FORM AND TEXTURE Plant form—or shape—and texture may not command as much attention as flower color does, but they are elements that shouldn't be overlooked. With some perennials, form and texture are *all* that really matters. For example, ferns don't flower, but what self-respecting moist shade garden would be without them? Clumps of curious young fiddleheads unfold in spring and change to lacy fronds that soften a shaded garden filled with the bolder shapes and textures. Hosta, coralbells, ornamental grasses, sedum, lamb's ears, and artemisia are also valued more for the form and texture of their foliage than they are for flowers.

The most interesting gardens contain plants with a wide assortment of shapes and textures. Some plants such as moneywort (*Lysimachia nummularia* 'Aurea') and bugleweed (*Ajuga reptans*) grow as ground-hugging mats and look good at the front of a garden.

Conversely, some plants have a loose, skirt-like form. Barrenwort (*Epimedium* spp.), lady's mantle (*Alchemilla mollis*), and catmint (*Nepeta* x *faassenii*) should be planted in front of taller, leggy plants to "skirt" their bare stems. Some plants have an airy cloudlike form and texture that you can see through—like a mist. The taller artemisias (*Artemisia* spp.), columbine (*Aquilegia* spp.), boltonia (*Boltonia asteroides*), baby's breath (*Gypsophila paniculata*), Russian sage (*Perovskia atriplicifolia*), and meadow rue (*Thalictrum* spp.) can visually lighten a garden that threatens to become too dense with bolder plants. Plants such as butterfly bush

Solomon's seal

(*Buddleia davidii*), old-fashioned bleeding heart (*Dicentra spectabile*), and variegated Solomon's seal (*Polygonatum odoratum* 'Variegatum') have graceful arching forms. Spiky plants such as blackberry lily (*Belamcanda flabellata*), cardinal flower (*Lobelia cardinalis*), foxglove (*Digitalis* spp.), gayfeather (*Liatris* spp.), hollyhock (*Alcea rosea*), and Siberian iris (*Iris sibirica*) are strongly vertical and can be used to break up rounded forms. Plants with rounded shapes include bloody cranesbill (*Geranium sanguineum*), hosta (*Hosta*), Bethlehem sage/lungwort (*Pulmonaria* spp.), and sedum 'Autumn Joy' (*Sedum* x 'Autumn Joy'). And in addition to ferns, perennials with feathery foliage such as astilbe (*Astilbe* spp.), threadleaf coreopsis (*Coreopsis verticillata*), flax (*Linum perenne*), and yarrow (*Achillea* spp.) help soften bolder plants with their filigreed leaves.

In some cases, plants may have two very different forms, depending on whether or not they are in bloom. In these instances, it is better to design a garden using the forms of the plants when they are out of flower.

While all of these variables might seem a bit overwhelming, there are a couple of easy ways to visualize how different forms and textures might look together. You can gauge how plants will look together by placing

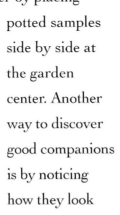

'Autumn Joy' sedum

potted samples side by side at the garden center. Another way to discover good companions is by noticing how they look together in other

Hydrangea bushes add garden structure.

people's gardens or in magazine and book photos. It's perfectly fine to copy a good idea!

GOOD COMPANIONS Most perennial gardens benefit from the addition of plants other than perennials. Trees, shrubs, vines, ornamental grasses, bulbs, and annuals can dramatically extend your garden's season of interest.

Many of the smaller trees and shrubs add structure to a perennial planting. This is especially relevant in regions with cold winters where herbaceous perennials go dormant for the winter and die back to the ground. Woody plants such as dogwood (*Cornus florida*), hydrangea (*Hydrangea* spp.), Japanese maple (*Acer palmatum*), redbud (*Cercis canadensis*), shrub roses (*Rosa* spp.), viburnum (*Viburnum* spp.), and witchhazel (*Hamamelis* spp.) also offer flowers and/or fall color.

Spring-blooming bulbs, and cold-tolerant annuals such as pansies and snapdragons, can add color early in the spring. A neat trick for disguising ripening bulb foliage that turns brown is to plant one daylily (*Hemerocallis*) in front of every clump of bulbs (five daffodils or tulips to one daylily is a good ratio). As the daylily leaves emerge they will cover the browning bulb foliage.

Annuals that enjoy warmer temperatures can be used to help fill out a new garden with young perennials that won't reach full size for another year or two. A few good choices include sweet alyssum (*Lobularia maritima*), blue salvia (*Salvia farinacea*), China pink (*Dianthus chinensis*), cosmos (*Cosmos bipinnatus*), larkspur (*Consolida ambigua*), melampodium (*Melampodium paludosum*), nicotiana (*Nicotiana* spp.), perilla (*Perilla frutescens*), spider flower (*Cleome hasslerana*), and Brazilian verbena (*Verbena bonariensis*).

Mixed gardens provide interest year-round.

GARDEN STYLE There are many different garden styles from which to choose. Therefore, it helps to have an initial idea of the general look you want your garden to take on. Cottage gardens, borders, island beds, rock gardens, and layered gardens are possible models.

Cottage gardens are loosely arranged with a cheerful mix of perennials and annuals. They grow over the years and have a very informal, homey feeling. They appear to be stuffed full of plants and are ever-ready to welcome and envelop visitors.

Borders are backed by a wall, fence, or a hedge or run adjacent to a walkway or path. Formal perennial borders are filled with well-behaved, painstakingly manicured plants. However, formal borders are quite labor-intensive and often fail because American gardeners try to use perennials that are better suited to a mild maritime English climate. A better choice is an informal border that is more

A butterfly garden is a joy in full bloom.

casually arranged with plants that are adapted to your growing conditions. A border that is adjacent to a path should not be more than 6 feet deep so that you can easily reach the sides. If a border is backed by a wall, fence, or hedge, a path should be constructed through the center of the border so you have easy access and so air can circulate readily.

Island beds are freestanding gardens surrounded by lawn. Island beds work best in large landscapes and they look most natural if there are several of them grouped together. Island beds can be quite large if you provide a path that allows access to the plants.

And if you have a natural rock outcropping, you might want to establish a rock garden.

Layered or mixed gardens are those that use small trees and shrubs, vines, and bulbs along with perennials. Layering is the arrangement of plants so that they are at least three deep. Layered plantings allow you to grow many plants in a limited space and they work very well in small yards. Trees and large shrubs typically occupy the back layer, smaller shrubs and large perennials make up the middle section, and smaller perennials, ground covers, select annuals and bulbs fill the front

A layered shade garden can become a backyard oasis.

space. In order to accomplish this, beds need to be a minimum of 6 feet wide.

PUT YOUR GARDEN ON PAPER While some people can design an entire perennial garden in their heads, most of us end up with better gardens if we commit a plan to paper. This easy six-step guide will help you get organized, make it easier to shop for plants, and give you direction when planting day comes.

1. Start with a simple sketch. Draw a quick outline of your garden bed noting its approximate dimensions and the amount of sun the area receives each day. Also list your favorite perennials so you'll be sure to include most, if not all, of them in your plan.

2. Look up your favorite perennials and jot down the colors they come in, their bloom

season, and their growth habits, including size. Note whether they prefer full sun, partial shade, or full shade. Specify how tall they grow.

3. If you only have a few favorites and a large space to fill, add a second list of plants you find attractive and that fit your conditions. Use plant catalogs to help you choose.

4. Use colored pencils to sketch planting sections within your bed outline. A more informal and interesting design will result if you vary the size and shape of these sections. Then decide which plants should go into each section of your plan. Be sure to include woody trees and shrubs if you plan to use them. Remember to keep tall plants in the back and low plants up front, filling in with intermediate heights. If a bed is going to be in an area where it will be seen from all sides, the tallest plants should be in the center of the bed with lower ones around the outer edges.

Vellum or tracing paper is helpful if you like to experiment with different ideas. Sheer vellum, available at art supply stores, allows you to lay a clean piece of paper over an old one so you can redraw a portion of the bed quickly.

5. As you plan, be sure flower colors in adjacent sections vary but don't clash. Maintain a balance of color in the bed. In large beds, repeat the same variety in several sections, making the sections larger than you would in small beds. In general, it's best to think in terms of odd quantities of plants—threes, fives, and sevens of a particular variety seem to work well. Once you've decided what will go in each section, double-check size, bloom time, and any other cultural requirements to make sure you haven't made a mistake. If you have, it's much easier to make changes on paper instead of in the garden after everything has been planted.

6. Once the plan is in its final form, you can then figure out approximately how many plants you'll need of each kind.

Careful planning will really benefit the perennials gardener in the long run. A sense of satisfaction will develop as your garden grows and your plans become a reality.

Balance color with shades of silver and green.

Chapter 4
PLANTING AND CARING FOR PERENNIALS

WHEN TO PLANT PERENNIALS Chapters 1 to 3 went through a lot of preliminaries: learning about different perennials, preparing the soil, selecting the garden site, and planning and designing the garden. Although you're just about ready to start digging, there are still a few options you must weigh.

You need to consider when you will do your planting and where you will purchase your plants. If, like many gardeners, you plan to plant in spring, it helps to know that you can begin planting bare-root and potted perennials about three weeks before your last frost date. This is the approximate date of the

'Elijah's Blue' ornamental fescue grass

last killing frost in the spring. Don't plant any earlier than this because the soil is generally wet and cold and plants will not develop new roots. If you haven't done so already, check with your local Cooperative Extension office or your favorite garden center to find out both your spring and fall frost dates. (The fall frost date is the approximate date of the first expected killing frost in autumn.)

You can continue planting pot-grown perennials until three or four weeks before hot summer temperatures hit. Don't plant after temperatures get above 80°F because roots need time to get established before plants are subjected to stressful high temperatures.

Northern gardeners with short growing seasons should stick with spring planting. Gardeners in Zones 5 and warmer can resume planting in late summer or early fall. Again, get all your perennials in the ground at least six weeks prior to the first killing fall frost. There are a few plants that should not be fall planted because they need a full growing season to get established prior to winter freezing and thawing. These include ornamental grasses, lavender, leadwort,

Stonecrop

dianthus, euphorbia, sedum, Russian sage, butterfly bush, blue mist spirea, and artemisia.

Avoid planting when your garden soil is wet. Wet soil is easily compacted and the soil structure is ruined when you walk on it. Also, oxygen, which is needed for root growth, is in short supply in wet soil.

PLANTING POTTED AND BARE-ROOT PERENNIALS Two major options exist for people purchasing new perennials. You can buy perennials from the local garden center or from a mail-order source. Garden centers usually sell perennials in one-quart pots (also called 4-inch), 1- or 2-gallon containers, and in bare-root form. A bare-root plant is sold without any soil around its roots. These plants have been grown in a field and the soil is removed from around the roots after they are dug up. Bare-root plants should be in a

dormant state when you get them. Mail-order suppliers usually sell bare-root plants and plants in 2- and 4-inch pots.

If you purchase plants in containers at a garden center, look for vigorous plants with multiple shoots and lush new growth. Stems should be sturdy and the plant should sit firmly in the pot. Avoid plants that are thin and wobbly. It's fine if a few roots poke through drainage holes in the bottom of the pot. However, never buy plants that are root-bound. Plants that have become rootbound can be identified by roots completely filling a pot and growing in profusion out of the holes in the bottom of the pot, and roots growing in circles around the inside of the pot. If you suspect that a plant has been in a pot for a long time and is rootbound, turn the pot over and gently remove the plant to inspect the roots. Healthy roots are white and grow downward. Root-bound plants have a solid mass of roots with very little soil showing.

Potted plants should feel sturdy and look healthy.

Containerized plants can be held for planting for several weeks if you keep them

watered and protected from inclement weather. Plant on a cloudy day or in the evening to eliminate stress from strong sun.

When you are ready to put plants in the ground, lay out or arrange the plants in the garden according to your planting plan or design. As you lay out plants, keep in mind their mature size, and space each plant so that neighboring plants barely touch. This will make your garden look full but it will also allow plenty of air to circulate so plants stay healthy. Start by placing the largest plants, such as ornamental grasses or shrubs and small trees if they are included in the design. Then work your way from one end of the garden to the other. Lay out all the plants before you dig any holes. This allows you to fine-tune plant placement easily.

Dig your planting holes one at a time. Make each hole slightly larger than the pot size you are planting. Carefully remove the plant from the pot by spreading your hand over the top of the pot. Stems and leaves will poke out between your fingers. Turn

Gently remove the plant from the pot.

the pot upside down and, with your free hand, pull the pot away from the plant. If the plant sticks, gently tap the rim against something solid to loosen the root ball from the sides of the pot.

If roots are tightly packed, gently loosen them with your fingers to encourage them to spread after planting. Otherwise, the roots may continue to grow in a tight mass. If they resist loosening, cut up the sides of the root ball in several places with a sharp knife or scissors, then loosen roots with your fingers.

Make sure you loosen the roots before planting.

Position the rootball in the planting hole so that the crown of the plant—where the plant meets the soil—is at the same depth it

Create a dam around newly planted perennials for watering.

was in the pot. If plants are placed too high they dry out easily. If placed too low, they sometimes fail to bloom and are subject to rot. Fan out the loosened roots and refill the hole with soil. Firm the soil around the crown and create a soil dam to hold water. Fill the dam with water, let it drain, and refill.

Bare-root plants are usually packed in some kind of moist medium and should be planted as soon as possible. Remove the packing medium and soak the plants in warm water for one hour prior to planting. Always keep the roots moist and away from wind and sun because they don't have any soil around them to protect them from drying out. Trim any extra long or damaged roots before planting. Set the plant in the planting hole so that the crown is at the

Trim any long or damaged roots from bare-root perennials before planting.

same depth it was previously. If the crown is not evident, as with bare-root peonies, plant so that the growth buds are 1 inch below the soil line. Spread the roots evenly over a mound of soil to help encourage well-rounded root growth. Fill in the soil firmly around roots, make a small dam, and water.

After planting, smooth the soil with a rigid steel, bowhead rake but be careful not to break any plants in the process. If you choose to use water-conserving soaker hoses or drip irrigation, lay them out on top of the soil and then cover with mulch. If you use an overhead watering system, simply mulch after the soil has been raked smooth.

WATERING Keep a close eye on all newly planted perennials during the first growing season. Many new perennials die because they get too much or too little water. The soil around their roots should be moist, but not soaking wet, for the first two weeks. For the next two weeks or so, water when the soil 2 inches below the surface is dry to the touch. After that, check the garden soil once a week and water if the soil is dry 3 or 4 inches deep.

To establish durable, deep root systems, water slowly and deeply rather than frequently and shallowly. A good rule of thumb is that many perennials grow well with 1 inch of water per week. The water can come from natural rainfall or from irrigation.

There's an easy way to calculate how long you have to run your watering system to apply 1 inch of water. Remove the tops from several small empty cans such as tuna cans. Wash them out and use a permanent marker to make a mark on the inside of the can 1 inch from the bottom. Dig holes 3 inches deep in various places around the garden and place the cans in the holes. Turn on your watering system and time how long it takes for the cans to fill with water to the 1 inch mark. This is how long you need to run your system to deliver 1 inch of water to your garden.

One of the best ways to water perennials in dry summer regions is with water-conserving soaker hoses. Water drips slowly onto the soil right around plant roots for several hours. All of the water soaks directly into the soil and down to plant roots without any waste. Additionally, because you are watering the soil and not the tops of plants, you greatly reduce the chance of disease problems that are common when leaves stay wet.

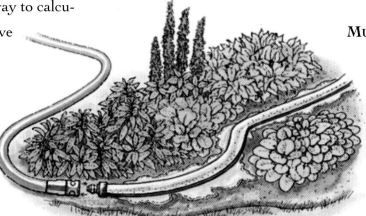

Using soaker hoses is an effective and efficient method of watering.

MULCHING Mulch is a material that is layered on top of the soil to conserve moisture, to moderate soil temperature, and to keep soil from crusting during drought and compacting from prolonged rain. It is also a tremendous time and labor saver because it greatly reduces the need for weeding. Mulch shades the soil, preventing many weed seeds from germinating. Weeds that do rise to the surface can be easily pulled.

Organic mulches are ideal for perennial gardens because they break down over time to improve the soil structure. Materials such as compost, well-rotted manure, shredded leaves, pine needles, and fine-textured bark chunks are good choices. You can make your own mulch by composting or by using a power tool called a shredder-chipper that turns yard waste into mulch.

A 2-inch layer of mulch should be spread over weed-free beds after planting, and if you use them, after soaker hoses have been set in place. Be careful to keep mulch pulled away from the crowns of plants. Crowns that are covered with moisture-holding mulch tend to rot. Organic mulches can be reapplied every spring if it is needed.

Mulch late summer- and fall-planted perennials with a 3- or 4-inch layer of mulch after the ground has frozen. Once the soil freezes you want it to stay that way so newly planted perennials aren't pushed out of the ground. These plants don't have mature root systems to keep them anchored during periods of alternate freezing and thawing. This is especially common in early spring when temperatures fluctuate widely. If you do find plants that have been forced (also known as "heaved") out of the ground, replant them immediately so they don't dry out and die.

One of the labor-saving benefits of easy-to-grow perennials is that they should be reliably winter hardy where you garden. If you have selected such plants, you shouldn't have to apply winter mulch after they are

'Mystique' irises

established. The exception to this is shallow-rooted perennials such as bearded iris and coralbells planted in northern Zone 1–4 gardens. These plants should get a 3- or 4-inch layer of mulch after the ground has frozen.

WEED CONTROL The key to long-term weed control is to be sure that your garden is free of weeds *before* you plant. After digging the soil in your planting area in early spring, wait a few weeks for weed seeds to germinate before planting. When unwanted seedlings arise, stir the top inch of soil and cut them down. Leave the lower soil, and the weed seeds imbedded there, undisturbed. Do this two or three times prior to planting and you will save yourself many hours of work later.

Try to remove the entire root of weeds to prevent regeneration.

If your garden is weed free at planting time and you apply an organic mulch to keep new "weedlings" from germinating, you will be able to keep up with weeds easily by patrolling the garden once or twice a week. It's easy to pull young weeds before they go to seed or start spreading. A sharp hoe and putty knife or fishtail weeder, sometimes called a dandelion fork, are great weeding tools. Use the hoe for shallow-rooted annual weeds. Use the putty knife or fishtail weeder for deep-rooted perennial weeds, being certain to dig and remove the entire root. If you don't get all of the root, it's likely that the weed will regenerate from the parts left in the soil.

Spacing your perennials closely also helps control weeds because the foliage of neighboring plants shades the ground and crowds out invaders. You need to be especially diligent about weeding in the spring when newly emerging perennials have not yet had a chance to canopy over the ground.

FERTILIZING Unfortunately, there's lots of misleading information about fertilizing perennials floating around. The truth is, most perennials are not heavy feeders and many actually respond negatively to over-fertilization. Our native coneflowers, black-eyed Susans, gayfeathers, and perennial sunflowers turn into

Purple coneflowers

"floppers" if they are force-fed. Other perennials grow leaves at the expense of flowers.

The best approach to "feeding" perennials is to incorporate plenty of organic matter

when the bed is prepared, then follow up with a 1- or 2-inch layer of compost in the spring. If you garden in the South you may need to apply a 3- or 4-inch layer of compost because organic matter and the resulting humus breaks down faster in hot, humid climates. Replenishing nutrients by applying them to the top of the soil around plants is known as top-dressing.

There are a few cases when quick-releasing inorganic fertilizers are beneficial. If you plant your garden while temperatures are cool, you need to remember that soil temperatures have to be warm before soil microbes can go to work turning organic matter into nutrient-rich humus. If this is the case, you might want to add a small amount of fast-acting inorganic fertilizer with a formula such as 5-10-5 or 10-10-10 to get your plants off to a good start. One pound of nitrogen per 1,000 square feet is sufficient. After temperatures rise, soil microbes will begin breaking down compost and sufficient nutrients will be released.

A second instance when you might want to use a fast-acting fertilizer is with perennials that are heavy feeders such as astilbe, Shasta daisy, delphinium, and repeat-blooming daylilies such as 'Stella d'Oro' and 'Happy Returns.' Again, one pound of nitrogen per 1,000 square feet can be applied to the soil around these plants in the spring. To give these hungry guys a mid-summer boost, you can apply a water-soluble foliar-feeding fertilizer with a 15-30-15 formula—especially if plants look chlorotic (discolored). Foliar fertilizers are poured or sprayed directly on leaves. The nutrients are immediately absorbed and available for plant use. Do this early on a cloudy day to prevent leaves from burning.

Some perennials appreciate a mid-summer application of foliar fertilizer.

ADDING NEW PLANTS TO AN ESTABLISHED PERENNIAL GARDEN Sometimes you can't—or don't want to—install a completely new garden. You may have an existing garden that needs reengineering. You may be faced with maturing trees that are turning what was once a sun garden into a shade garden. Or you may have read about improved varieties of plants you are currently growing. Or it just may be the case that you are tempted to try something new. Possibly, your garden looks tired and needs a facelift. If any of these scenarios describes your situation, read on.

In most cases, you will probably have to remove some plants from your garden in order to make room for new ones. As you consider which plants stay and which plants go, prime candidates for removal are those that are infested by hard-to-control weeds such as crabgrass, wild garlic, goosegrass,

Lupine, lavender, and delphinium ready for planting

nutsedge, and wild violets. Other plants that should be on the list for removal are those that are regularly plagued by disease or insects. Garden phlox and bee balm that are disfigured every year by powdery mildew should be replaced with newer mildew-resistant varieties. And bearded irises that are plagued by

Siberian iris

borers can be replaced with Siberian irises, which borers do not bother.

Before you begin renovating a bed, spread a tarp on the grass next to where you are working to receive plants taken out of the garden. The tarp will catch loose soil and make cleanup much easier. A spading fork with wide tines or a square-edged spade are good tools for digging and lifting perennials. If you plan to replant, keep the plants moist and shaded while they are out of the ground. If plants will be out of the garden for more than one day, pot them temporarily in plastic containers until they are ready for replanting.

If you plan to dispose of a plant, simply wheel it to the compost pile. Don't feel compelled to keep a plant that you don't like or that, despite your best efforts, doesn't grow well in your garden. There are too many wonderful perennials available to put up with something that doesn't please you. And think twice before you give a reject to a friend or neighbor—will they be happy with it if you weren't?

If you like a plant but want to reduce the amount of space it occupies in the garden, division is in order. Division is the process where plants are separated or split apart to make more plants or to reinvigorate an old plant that isn't performing well. See Chapter 5, pages 74–76 for detailed instructions on how to divide perennials.

Weed control and soil improvement are just as important when adding plants to an established garden as they are in new gardens. As mentioned earlier, remove plants that are overrun by weeds. Don't replant them unless you are absolutely certain you have eliminated every bit of the weed's root and washed away any seeds that may be lodged in the crown of the desirable plant. Then, thoroughly weed the soil surrounding the area of the removed plant.

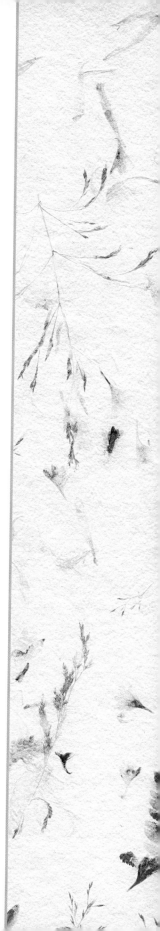

Fill open garden areas with fresh perennials.

Don't even think of replanting or adding new plants until you add organic matter to the soil. Fill an empty 2-pound coffee can with compost and mix it with the soil where you are planting. Then top-dress the entire garden with 2 inches of compost. As the com-post breaks down, it will improve soil structure and feed your plants.

GROOMING AND MAINTAINING PERENNIALS

Once perennials are established, they require minimal maintenance. That's one of their big advantages: The plants simply keep coming back each growing season for as long as they're kept healthy and vigorous.

This doesn't mean, of course, that no care at all is needed. None of the jobs you'll do to keep perennials in peak condition require a great deal of time and energy when taken individually. Some things you'll simply do as you walk along—pause to pull out a stray weed or snap off a dead flower. Chores such as mulching, which require special preparation or equipment, you can do when you have extra time available.

These few simple care practices will keep perennials looking their best and keep your plants in bounds.

THINNING Sometimes you need to reduce the density of a plant by cutting out shoots or stems at ground level—otherwise known as

Frikart's aster

thinking. This is done to get more light into the center of a plant, to promote better air circulation, or to improve the general shape of a plant. Plants prone to powdery mildew, such as asters, garden phlox, and bee balm, usually benefit from thinning in the spring. You can also thin low-growing perennials such as bugleweed, Bethlehem sage, and lamb's ears in the summer when high humidity threatens to rot the crown of plants.

DEADHEADING This rather fierce term refers to removing faded flowers from plants. If left to their own devices, many perennials bloom gloriously for a short period of time. Then they stop flowering and set seed.

Deadheading interrupts this cycle. If faded flowers are removed before they set seed, many will send out another flush of blooms to try to complete the reproductive cycle. The blooms in the second display may not be as large or as numerous as the first, but they are certainly worth the effort. Other perennials that bloom over an extended period of time benefit from deadheading because it increases the number of flowers that are produced and the length of time over which they are produced. Deadheading also gives you some control over flowers that can be invasive because they self-seed. Blackberry lily, goldenrod, hollyhock, valerian, purple coneflower, black-eyed Susan, and summer phlox self-seed with abandon if they aren't deadheaded.

Basically, there are two places to make deadheading cuts. With perennials that have leaves along the flower stem, cut just above the point where you see a new shoot or bud emerging. This is usually in the axil of the set of leaves closest to the old flower.

Deadhead spent blooms to encourage new growth.

'Biedermeier' columbine

To deadhead perennials that don't have leaves along their flower stems, make the cut at the bottom of a flowering stem near the base of the plant. Remove the flowering stems of plants such as coralbells, hosta, lady's mantle, barrenwort, and Bethlehem sage by cutting the stem at the base of the plant after all the flowers are spent.

CUTTING BACK This technique is used to keep leggy plants more compact, to promote new foliage growth, or to coerce plants to bloom repeatedly. Sometimes you can avoid staking tall plants that are prone to flopping, such as tall asters and boltonia, if you cut them back by about one-half in early summer. This keeps plants shorter than normal and eliminates the need for staking. Other plants such as spring-blooming dianthus and moss phlox should be cut back by one-half after they bloom to prevent them from opening up in the center or getting scraggly. Still other

plants such as columbine, Shasta daisy, goldenrod, hardy salvia, and yarrow should be cut back to the basal foliage (leaves that grow from the crown or base of the plant) after they finish flowering. This will promote lush new foliage growth and, sometimes, another round of flowers.

SHOVEL DIVIDING This maintenance practice keeps vigorous perennials in their allotted space. As you stroll the garden looking for weeds and spent flowers, keep an eye out for perennials that are encroaching on their neighbors. When you spot plants that are getting out of hand, insert a round-point digging shovel into the plant with the back of the shovel against what you want to keep and the front of the shovel next to what you want to remove. Pull back on the shovel and pop the unwanted portion of the plant out of the ground. This method works well on spreading perennials that are still blooming

'Peter Pan' solidago

strongly and show no other signs of being overcrowded.

DIVISION It is often necessary to revitalize perennials that have been in the ground for three years or more by division. Good reasons to divide include:

    ⚘ reduced flowering (either in size or quantity)

    ⚘ bare spots in the center of a clump (all of the growth takes place in a ring around the outer edges)

    ⚘ stems that were once stout and self-supporting flop

    ⚘ plants that are crowding out neighboring plants

    ⚘ to move part of the plant to another area of the garden

    ⚘ to give part of a plant away to a fellow gardener

Yellow coneflower seed heads

Most herbaceous perennials need to be cut back before winter.

See Chapter 5, pages 74–76 for detailed instructions on how to divide perennials.

PREPARING FOR WINTER If you've selected perennials that are winter hardy in your area, there's really very little you need do to get the garden ready for winter. Once frost hits, the top growth of most perennials will die back to the ground. When this occurs, use hand pruners to cut off the dead stems, leaving only the bottom 2 or 3 inches. Remove this material, along with any other garden debris you collect, and place in your compost pile. Dead plant matter left in the garden over the winter could harbor overwintering disease organisms and pests.

There are a few easy-to-grow perennials that you don't want to cut back until spring. These include semi-woody plants such as butterfly bush, blue mist spirea, and lavender.

Likewise, refrain from cutting back plants that offer winter interest such as ornamental grasses, sedum, and the flower heads of black-eyed Susan, which will feed birds for several more months. Be sure, too, to leave hellebores, Japanese spurge, dianthus, and any other evergreen perennials standing.

If rainfall is in short supply, continue deep watering until the ground is frozen. If plants go into winter with dry roots, they're likely to suffer badly from winter sun and wind. The last thing you will want to do is to apply a winter mulch to late summer- and fall-planted perennials and shallow-rooted plants (see pages 52–53).

There are many ways to stake plants if you do find that staking is needed; the best method depends on the plant in question.

Apply a layer of winter mulch over cut-back perennials.

Metal support stakes can be used year after year.

PERIPHERAL STAKING This is when all the stems are supported at once by placing some kind of cage around the perimeter of a plant. There are many variations on this theme including peony rings, metal linking stakes, metal tomato cages with the top ring removed and inserted into the ground upside down, four bamboo stakes positioned around a clump of foliage and tied together with jute, and pea staking, where branches of fine twiggy shrubs are cut and inserted around light, airy plants such as baby's breath to keep them from splitting apart in the center and laying down.

SINGLE STAKES Materials such as bamboo or rebar work well for staking

Single stakes work best with plants that have tall, individual stems.

long-stemmed plants such as lilies and delphinium. Drive the stake into the ground 6 inches away from the center of the plant to avoid impaling the crown of the plant. Use a stake that is three-fourths the expected height of the stems (plus 6 inches for the portion of the stake that is underground). As the stem grows, tie it to the stake every 12 inches or so with jute. Twist the jute between the stem and the stake so the plant doesn't rub against the stake. The last tie should be just below the bottom of the flower head.

Regardless of the method you use, be sure to get your stakes in place early in the growing season. Stakes placed early are readily covered by expanding foliage

Staked delphinium

and are much less conspicuous than stakes placed late in the season. Be sure, too, to insert stakes at least 6 inches into the ground, to prevent them from toppling over due to the weight of the plants they are supporting.

PESTS AND OTHER PROBLEMS If you take care to select easy-to-grow perennials and provide them with the best possible growing conditions, your garden will flourish. However, you will probably encounter a few insects or a disease sooner or later. Consult the table on pages 64–68 to help you identify the most common garden pests and diseases. If you need more help, take a specimen to a horticulturist at your local garden shop or your county Cooperative Extension office to have it identified. Early and accurate detection is the key to successfully controlling problems. If you catch the problem when it first appears, chances are you will be able to get rid of it quickly and it won't return.

Once you have identified the problem, you need to decide how to control it.

STAKING PERENNIALS

If grown properly, most easy-to-care-for perennials are self-supporting and do not require special staking to keep them upright. Occasionally though, plants get a little too tall and flop over, as will boltonia and some of the taller yarrows. One way to get around this is to select shorter-growing cultivars such as *Boltonia asteroides* 'Nana,' which grows 24 inches tall instead of *B. asteroides* 'Snowbank,' which reaches heights of 4 to 5 feet. Sometimes large, multi-petaled flower heads such as double peonies become heavy after a rain and droop—and then they need staking. Remedy this by selecting peony varieties that have fewer petals such as single, anemone, or semi-double forms.

Sometimes, though, staking cannot be avoided. Gardeners who live in regions with heavy summer rain or where gusting wind is common will probably have to stake choice plants. Overly rich soil may cause some plants to get tall and lanky and sun-loving plants that receive too much shade stretch for more sunlight.

When an infestation is slight, you can simply remove the sick plants or the offending insects. Sometimes a blast from the garden hose is all that's needed to dislodge intruders. For advanced problems or heavy infestations, you'll probably need to turn to insecticides or fungicides, available in both organic and inorganic forms.

Using environmentally safe, organic products is an excellent way to encourage a healthy garden and to keep your surroundings free from harmful chemicals. The application of garden pesticides is definitely an area where the "more is better" attitude is out of place. If your problem is of such proportion that you must apply pesticides, do so in the evening to avoid harming pollinating bees and butterflies. Use organic products such as pyrethrin that kill quickly and then break down without leaving a harmful residue. Other products, such as *Bacillus thuringiensis* (Bt for short)—a bacterial disease that only harms caterpillars—target one specific pest and ignore other beneficial insects such as ladybugs and spiders.

One final note: New biological and chemical controls are continually being developed. Effective new products are unveiled every year while some toxic inorganic products are taken off the market. Therefore, it is very important to correctly identify your pest or disease problem and to consult with your county extension agent or the horticulturist at your local garden shop. They can usually recommend the best available product for controlling your particular problem.

INSECTS AND ANIMALS

SYMPTOM	CAUSE	CURE	PLANTS
Cluster of small, soft-bodied insects on buds and growth tips (gray, black, pink, or green in color); sticky secretions may be evident	aphids	Spray with a blast of water, insecticidal soap, or pyrethrin in evening	black-eyed Susan, chrysanthemum, daylily, geraniums (hardy), lily, lupine, peony, Shasta daisy, sedum
Leaves chewed away; hard-shelled beetles on plant and burrowed into flowers	beetles and bugs of various kinds	Hand pick if populations are low; if present in large numbers, apply rotenone; spray with insecticidal soap or neem oil; apply milky spore to lawns to control Japanese beetle grubs; dust plants with carbaryl (Sevin*[1]).	Japanese anenome, aster, coreopsis, hollyhock, lupine, peony, garden phlox, Oriental poppy
Growth tips wilted; small hole in plant stem at point where wilting begins	borers	Make a vertical slit in the stem, remove the borer and smash it; insert wires into stems to kill borers or inject beneficial nematodes into the holes; discard badly infested plants	columbine, delphinium, hollyhock, iris, lily
Leaves and stems chewed; insects seen hopping and flying	grasshopper	Pick off by hand and crush; treat young grasshoppers and their nests with a protozoan pathogen called *Nosema locustae*	catmint, daylily, ornamental grasses, salvia, yarrow

[1] = inorganic treatment

* = copyrighted brand name

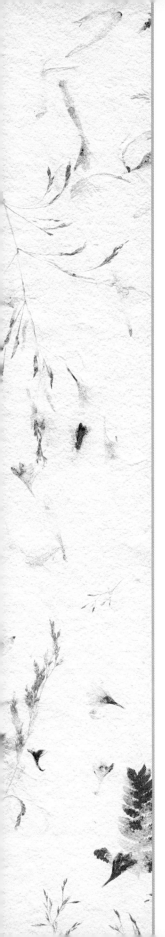

Insects and Animals *(continued)*

Symptom	Cause	Cure	Plants
Leaves peppered with small, round holes; small, triangular-shaped bugs seen when disturbed	 leafhoppers	Tolerate light damage; keep garden free of weeds; if severe, try repeated applications of insecticidal soap; spray neem oil or other refined horticultural oil on plants; grow small-flowered nectar plants, such as sweet alyssum and scabiosa to attract beneficial insects such as assassin bugs, lacewings, and parasitic flies to help control leafhoppers.	aster, baby's breath, chrysanthemum
Leaves "painted" with whitish, curling trails	 Leaf miners	Leaf miner damage is rarely fatal; remove infested leaves and spray with an insecticide containing malathion; place plastic sheeting under infested plants and disguise it with a topping of organic mulch	chrysanthemum, columbine, Shasta daisy
Plants entirely gone or eaten down to small stubs; evidence of animal tracks or droppings	 rabbits or deer	Spray with Hinder*[1] or other repellents; fence out rabbits with 3' high chicken wire or other close-woven fencing; surround garden with battery charged fencing for deer	hosta, lily

[1] = inorganic treatment

* = copyrighted brand name

SYMPTOM	CAUSE	CURE	PLANTS
Silvery slime trails on plants; soft sticky slugs on plants after dark (check with flashlight); holes eaten in leaves	slugs and snails	Set out shallow containers of beer; make barriers of diatomaceous earth; set out metaldehyde slug bait[1]; pick by hand after dark or on dark days	bleeding heart, delphinium, hosta, lupine
Leaves yellowing with speckled look; fine spider webs on backs of leaves and at point where leaves attach to stem; very tiny bugs on backs of leaves	spider mites	Irrigate to keep soil moist since spider mites are common during hot, dry weather. Treat plants with insecticidal soap as soon as they leaf out. Beneficial predatory mites can be released to feed on damaging mites. Use a commercial miticide[1] if populations get completely out of hand	daylily, garden phlox
Brown or white flecks on plant leaves	thrips	Spray with insecticidal soap, pyrethrins, or neem	chrysanthemum, daylily, foxglove, iris, peony

[1] = inorganic treatment

DISEASES

SYMPTOM	CAUSE	CURE	PLANTS
Leaves and flowers turn mushy and smell rotten	bacterial soft rot	Dig infected plants and discard; make new plantings in raised beds or improve drainage by working 2 to 4 inches of compost or other organic matter into the soil	daylily, iris
Leaves have spots with purple or yellow-green margins	fungal leaf spot	Remove and discard diseased leaves; keep foliage dry; if the infection persists, apply sulphur, an organically acceptable fungicide	columbine, purple cone-flower, coralbells, fox-glove, hollyhock, iris
Leaves rot off at ground level; plants wilt or topple over	various fungal rots (crown, root, stem, and Southern blight)	Remove and destroy diseased plants as soon as possible; discard the sur-rounding 6 inches of soil; treat the soil where the plant once grew with ammonium nitrate, a nitrogenous fertilizer; apply sulfur, an organically accept-able fungicide; avoid overwatering; if the disease is severe and widespread, apply a fungicide with the active chemical ingre-dient quintozene[1]	bellflower, black-eyed Susan, bleeding heart, coralbells, delphinium, hollyhock, hosta, iris, garden phlox, sedum

[1] = inorganic treatment

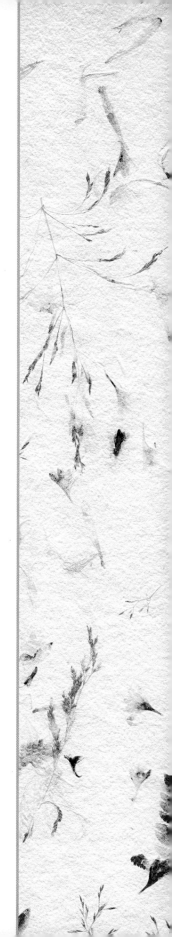

DISEASES *(continued)*

SYMPTOM	CAUSE	CURE	PLANTS
Lower leaves and stems turn grayish and look slightly wilted	powdery mildew	Increase air circulation; spray with sulfur or antitranspirant	aster, astilbe, bee balm, coralbells, coreopsis, lupine, garden phlox, Oriental poppy
Orange or reddish-brown raised dots form on backs of leaves; leaves look wilted	rust	Increase air circulation; keep foliage dry; buy rust-resistant varieties; spray flowers with sulfur	aster, bellflower, hollyhock, iris, lupine, sedum
Leaves become mottled, curl, and shrivel; plants become deformed	virus	Remove and destroy plants; buy blight resistant strains; control disease-carrying aphids and leaf hoppers; wash hands after handling plants	purple coneflower, lily
Leaves wilt and turn yellow; entire plant shuts down and dies	wilt	Remove infected plants and destroy; buy wilt-resistant varieties	astilbe, bellflower, dianthus, foxglove, salvia

Chapter 5
PROPAGATION

PROPAGATION IS THE PRACTICE of making new plants from old plants. If you've never done it before, you'll be thrilled to discover how easy it is to propagate most plants.

To have a bountiful supply of inexpensive plants all it takes is a little attention to how plants grow and some time in the garden collecting seed, dividing plants, or taking cuttings. As with all young creatures, you'll need to take good care of your newly started plants.

HOW PLANTS REPRODUCE Most plants can be propagated using simple methods. The key to success is knowing how a particular plant reproduces naturally and then taking advantage of that tendency.

Flowering plants reproduce most commonly by setting seed which reaches the soil,

Lupine

germinates, and grows into new plants. Most of these new plants differ in appearance and/or growth habit from the plant that produced the seed. This is because seed is produced sexually. That is, two parents contribute genetic material to the new offspring. You can propagate some perennials by saving seed from plants in your garden or by purchasing seed from commercial sources. Seed is either sown directly where you want it to grow in the garden, or started in flats then transplanted to the garden.

Other plants reproduce vegetatively (also called asexually) by forming new plants directly from the mother plant. Unlike seed production, new plants look exactly like the parent plants. As far as propagation goes, division and cuttings are the two easiest vegetative methods. Peren-

nials that form clumps of shoots and multiple roots can be quickly and easily propagated by division. Cuttings can be taken from some perennials by removing pieces of plant stems or roots. These pieces then grow into whole new plants that look like the parent plant.

STARTING PERENNIALS FROM SEED Some perennials are good candidates for seed propagation. Perennials that are especially well adapted to the region where you garden, such as woodland wildflowers in the Pacific Northwest and native prairie flowers and grasses in the Midwest, are good bets. Relatively short-lived perennials that tend to reseed themselves in the garden can also be easily seed-propagated by gardeners.

All seeds have a similar need for soil, moisture, light, and nutrients to grow into healthy plants.

Seeds sown in flats or containers must have good drainage and loose, light soil to germinate. For this reason, a sterile, soilless medium produces the best results. Peat-based mixes made especially for starting seeds or a 1:1:1 mixture of vermiculite, perlite,

and milled sphagnum moss (not coarse peat moss) work well.

Almost any kind of container works as long as it has drainage holes and is at least 3 or 4 inches deep. Styrofoam containers, plastic or aluminum salad bar containers, plastic-coated milk cartons with the tops cut off, reusable plastic flats or pots, and peat pots will all work well. Be sure to scrub and sterilize previously used containers with a mild bleach solution and rinse well.

Moisten your germinating mixture with water thoroughly before sowing your seed. Make sure to keep it evenly moist until seedlings emerge. Never let the soil dry out but don't keep it soggy. You can cover your containers with plastic wrap to keep moisture

Many perennials can be started from seed.

EASY PERENNIALS TO GROW FROM SEED

Baby's breath	Delphinium
Blackberry lily	Hollyhock
Blanket flower	Jupiter's beard
Butterfly weed	Lupine
Columbine	Oriental poppy
Coreopsis	Sunflowers
Shasta daisy	Sweet william

in. Be sure to remove the cover as seeds begin to sprout to avoid disease problems.

Water gently so you don't pound the seed into the soil. After seedlings emerge, water less often. When seedlings are a few inches tall let the top half-inch of the growing mixture dry out between waterings.

Many seeds need heat to germinate. In general, seeds germinate readily in 75°F soil. (That's soil temperature, not air temperature.) Place seed trays where the soil will warm, such as on top of your refrigerator, water heater, or television. Incandescent light bulbs placed near flats are also a good way to

generate heat. A soil-heating cable can be purchased at garden centers or by mail order if you are starting a large number of plants that need supplemental heat. Windowsills are not a good choice for seed germination because nighttime temperatures and air leaks around glass are too cold for proper seed growth. Once seedlings emerge, air temperature between 65°F and 75°F is adequate.

Most seeds don't need light to germinate but seedlings need plenty of light to flourish. Where there is not enough natural light available—a common problem in climates where winter clouds fill the sky for weeks—seedlings become leggy and pale and stretch toward the closest light source. To avoid this, raise seedlings under fluorescent lights.

Use a pair of 4- to 6-foot-long fluorescent shop tubes in a fixture that hangs from

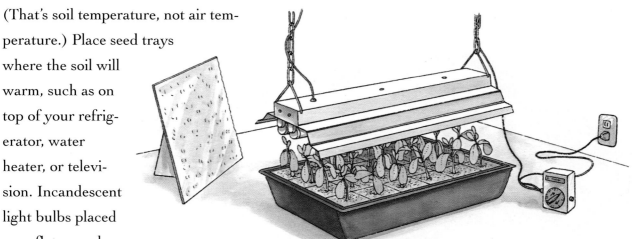

Even, bright light is key when seedlings start to sprout.

chains. Chains and cup hooks will allow you to raise or lower the height of the lights based on the height of your seedlings. Position the light so it is 4 to 6 inches above the plants. One shop light fixture provides enough light for two full size flats.

CARING FOR SEEDLINGS In addition to the previous tips, there are a few other key facets of growing seedlings that you should know. As seedlings grow, they benefit from fertilization, thinning or transplanting, and hardening off.

Seeds and young plants contain all the nutrients they need to get going, but older

Coreopsis

plants need additional nutrients for healthy growth. Start fertilizing seedlings with water-soluble all-purpose fertilizers or fish emulsion when they develop their first true sets of leaves. The first leaves that emerge from a seed are seed leaves, also called cotyledons—the next set is the first set of true leaves. Apply a half strength fertilizer solution once or twice a week for the first three weeks and then increase to full strength until plants go in the ground.

If seedlings are crowded, thin them by snipping off weak seedlings at soil level with small, sharp scissors. Then go back and thin extra seedlings by cutting them off so the remaining plants won't have leaves touching or roots growing into each other when they are big enough to transplant into the garden.

If you grow a lot of seedlings in a flat they must be transplanted to larger containers before planting outdoors. Transplant them as soon as the first true set of leaves develop. If you wait longer, the seedlings' roots are likely to get tangled and they will be damaged as you pry them apart. To avoid damage, handle individual plants by the cotyledons—not by the true leaves, stem, or roots.

Harden off your seedlings when they are big enough by setting containers outside in a lightly shaded, sheltered spot. Set plants out for a few hours at first, gradually increasing the amount of time they spend outdoors and the amount of sun they receive. Transplant to the garden on a cloudy day that isn't windy, to reduce shock. Water well and provide temporary shade if transplants wilt.

SOWING SEEDS DIRECTLY IN THE GARDEN

A seedbed for starting perennials should be raked smooth and have all dirt clumps broken so that a fine, even surface is formed. Dig shallow furrows using the side of a trowel or a thin board. Furrows should vary in depth according to seed size—they should be about three times the size of the seed to be planted.

Drop individual seeds into the furrow, spacing them ¼ to ½ inch apart. Cover them with fine, crumbled soil. Cover the seeds to a depth of two to three times their diameter. Very fine seeds require no covering.

Newly planted seeds should be watered very carefully with a fine spray—use a small bulb sprinkler or something similar to avoid displacing the soil or seeds. From the time they are planted until the young seedlings have formed their second set of true leaves, they are most vulnerable to drying out. Be sure to check the seedbed several times a day, spraying the seeds with a fine water spray as needed to keep the soil moist but not soaked.

When the seedlings reach the stage where they have their second set of true leaves, thin them by pulling out the extra seedlings so they're spaced 6 inches apart. These can be replanted elsewhere, given to other gardeners, or thrown away.

Oriental poppies

Some perennial seeds can be sown directly outside.

DIVISION Many perennials need to be divided regularly to flower and grow well. The frequency of division depends on the kind of perennial, its age, and how rapidly you want to spread it around the garden. A natural by-product of plant division is additional plants, which can be replanted in other parts of your own yard or shared with other gardeners.

Everywhere but in the South, the best time to divide most perennials is early spring when the foliage is 3 inches tall. However,

WHEN TO DIVIDE PERENNIALS

Many perennials should be divided every three to five years. Others can go longer. You will know it's time to divide if flowers are fewer or smaller, bare spots develop in the center of a clump, plants that used to be compact get leggy and flop over, plants spread too much, or they develop disease due to overcrowding.

EVERY 1 TO 3 YEARS

Ajuga
Aster

Astilbe
Bee balm
Blackberry lily
Black-eyed Susan
Coreopsis
Delphinium
Dianthus
Daylily, ever-blooming
(*Hemerocallis,* such as
'Stella de Oro' and
'Happy Returns')

Foxglove
Iris, bearded
Phlox
Shasta daisy
Yarrow

EVERY 4 TO 5 YEARS

Coralbells
Gayfeather

Geranium, hardy
Goldenrod
Joe Pye weed
Once-blooming daylily
Purple coneflower

EVERY 6 TO 10 YEARS

Bethlehem sage
Heartleaf brunnera

Hosta
Lady's mantle
Oriental poppy
Siberian iris

ALMOST NEVER NEED DIVISION

Baby's breath
Butterfly weed
Goat's beard
Hardy hibiscus
Lenten rose
Japanese anemone
Peony

there are a few exceptions, such as perennials that flower in early spring. Divide early-spring bloomers such as moss phlox right after they've finished blossoming. In warm climates—such as in the South—fall is a better time to divide perennials. Another exception is bearded iris. This perennial should be divided in late summer while it is semi-dormant. And there are a few fleshy-rooted plants—peonies, Oriental poppies, and Siberian irises —which, even though they bloom in summer, do better if they're divided in the fall, approximately one month before the first frost.

Divide rhizomes with a sharp knife.

There are several techniques for dividing perennials. They can be divided by taking pieces away from their outer edges—separating them from the main plant by cutting through the crown with a knife or a sharp-bladed spade. You can also lift the entire plant from the ground and pull or cut it apart. Dig 10 inches away from the outside edge of the clump to ensure that you get all of the root system. Remove the entire clump from the ground and keep it shaded and moist while it is out of the ground. Some plants such as aster and bee balm divide very easily. They're loosely interwoven and can be separated into chunks simply by pulling them apart with your hands. Large clumps such as astilbe, daylily, and hosta can be divided with a sharp, flat-edged spade. Others are so tightly held together that it becomes a real challenge to break them up. Fortunately, the tough ones are also very hardy and will survive even if you ultimately have to resort to using a meat cleaver or machete! Japanese irises, lupines, and goat's beard fall into this latter category.

Some perennials have large, fleshy under-ground stems called rhizomes. Bearded irises are one example. To divide these types, dig up the entire clump and shake out the dirt. Then use a sharp knife to cleanly cut them into smaller clumps containing three or more buds. Let the pieces air-dry for about an hour

Joe Pye weed

so the wounds can seal over before replanting them.

The primary concerns here are to keep as many of the roots intact as possible and to have some roots and some foliage in each division. If you are dividing in spring as new growth is emerging, you won't need to trim back foliage. If you are dividing later in the season after leaves have grown in size and number, cut back the foliage by at least one-half to reduce moisture loss from the leaves. Leave three to five growth buds per division. Decide which divisions to keep and which to toss in the compost heap. Toss divisions with fewer than three buds and those with sparse roots. Avoid the impulse to get as many separate clumps as possible. Larger clumps will thrive, while small divisions are likely to struggle and grow very slowly.

Add organic matter to the planting hole and always plant the new divisions at the same depth as they were growing before lifting. Firm the soil around each new plant and water well to help settle the soil closely around the roots. The addition of enough water-soluble fertilizer to make a weak feeding solution will help get the new plants off to a good start. If nature doesn't provide adequate water during the first several weeks after division, be sure to water deeply as needed.

CUTTINGS Like division, stem and root cuttings will produce new plants exactly like their parents. Not all perennials will generate whole new plants from pieces of themselves, although many do this easily.

Herbaceous stem cuttings can be taken when plants are growing but are not blooming. Mid- to late summer is a good time to gather cut-

Bee balm

tings because you won't need supplemental heat to get plants to root. Additionally, plants have many stems to cut from in summer and are often in need of pruning to restore a handsome shape.

Some plants root better if cuttings are taken when new shoots expand in the spring. If some of your cuttings don't root well the first time, try taking cuttings earlier in the season the following year. Another reason to take cuttings earlier in the season is to get new plants from hardy perennials that can be transplanted to the garden that same year.

Stem cuttings should be taken from the active growing tips of the plant. Cuttings should be between 3 and 6 inches in length,

GOOD CANDIDATES FOR STEM CUTTINGS

Bee balm	Geranium
Bellflower	Phlox
Butterfly bush	Russian sage
Chrysanthemum	Sedum
Dianthus	Yarrow

and removed from the parent plant in the evening or in the early morning when they're in peak condition. Use only healthy plants that are free from insects and diseases and are in an active growing stage.

Gather cuttings for only five minutes, bringing them indoors to process immediately. This will cut down on the possibility of wilting and the energy loss that accompanies it. After one batch of cuttings has been completed, you can gather additional batches, preparing each

Take stem cuttings from healthy plants. Then, before rooting, remove side shoots and leaves from the cutting.

Good Candidates for Root Cuttings

Japanese anemone   Geranium
Bleeding heart   Oriental poppy
Butterfly weed   Solomon's seal

and inserting the cuttings into the rooting medium before picking a new group.

Rooting hormone powder—which you apply to the end of the cutting to help it root—is favored by some gardeners, but it is not absolutely essential. However, hormone powders do speed up the rooting process and generally help produce a higher percentage of successful "takes." The powder is long lasting and inexpensive—the smallest packet you can buy is probably all you'll need for hundreds of cuttings.

A rooting medium must provide good drainage and air circulation. At the same time, it must supply support to the plant stems and enough compaction to keep the stems moist. Coarse sand is the traditional rooting medium, but most growers today use some combination of sand, vermiculite, perlite, and peat moss. A mix of perlite combined with an equal amount of either peat moss or vermiculite provides good drainage and moisture retention.

Always make a hole first before inserting the prepared cutting into the medium. Firm the medium around the stem. Once all the cuttings are inserted, water them to help them settle into the medium, covering them with a plastic bag to form a tent. The cutting leaves should not come in contact with the plastic. If they do, this is a prime environment for rot that will kill the cuttings. To avoid this problem, insert stakes in the medium in such a way that they will hold the plastic away from the cuttings.

Place the pots with cuttings in an outdoor area sheltered from direct sun and wind. The north side of a building is a good choice. Cuttings can be rooted indoors but disease problems tend to increase because indoor air does not circulate as well. Keep the growing medium moist but not soggy. Cuttings are

A makeshift greenhouse can aid in rooting stem cuttings.

Root cuttings grow very slowly.

susceptible to rot so watch them carefully and reduce water if necessary. Most cuttings root easily and should be ready for potting into larger containers in two to four weeks. Test their readiness by pulling gently on the cutting. If they resist, they are probably well rooted.

Another method of propagation is taking root cuttings. For just two or three root cuttings, simply dig down beside the parent plant and cut off one or two roots with a knife or hand pruners. For a larger number of root cuttings, dig up the parent plant and trim off all of the side roots. Discard the parent plant, or trim the top back heavily and replant it.

In general, root cuttings of summer- and fall-flowering perennials should be taken in the spring. However, Japanese anemone cuttings should be taken in late winter or very early spring. Cuttings of spring-flowering plants—such as bleeding heart and Oriental poppy—should be taken in the fall. To help identify the top of the cutting (that part closest to the plant's main root or crown) from the bottom, make cuts straight across the top end and a slanted cut at the bottom end of each segment. Cut fine roots into 1-inch lengths. Cut fleshy roots into 1½- to 2-inch pieces.

Cuttings of fine roots can be scattered horizontally over the surface of the rooting medium (rich sandy loam is best) and covered with about ½ inch of soil or sand. Fleshy roots are planted upright in the medium, 2 to 3 inches apart, with the top ¼ inch of the cutting sticking out of the ground.

Unlike stem cuttings that root within weeks, root cuttings are slow to generate new top growth. Keep them in a sunny location out of direct sun, and continue to water them whenever the rooting medium begins to dry.

Fragrant Solomon's seal

THREE GARDEN DESIGNS

Garden designs are usually as unique as each individual gardener. Take a look at these designs, use some of their elements, and stimulate some brainstorms of your own. Each of these gardens was designed with a general theme—and growing conditions—in mind. Remember to check each plant's requirements carefully.

The "General Perennial Garden" will suit most any sunny and partly sunny yard. It works well as a front yard display that welcomes visitors and beautifies the neighborhood.

The "Butterfly Garden" is designed to attract birds and insects—especially butterflies. A sunny spot, food for butterfly larvae, and good sources of nectar are the keys to this garden's success.

The "Backyard Shade Garden" features three layers for different levels of shade. This informal garden adds depth to a small yard and becomes an instant getaway.

GENERAL PERENNIAL GARDEN

Lightly shaded bed by tree: columbine (*Aquilegia* spp.); lily (*Lilium* spp.); forget-me-not (*Myosotis sylvatica*)

Tree: honey locust (*Gleditsia triacanthos inermis*)

Center sunny area: goldenrod (*Solidago* hybrids); aster (*Aster* spp.)

Center bush: boltonia (*Boltonia asteroides*)

Sunny bed: orange coneflower (*Rudbeckia fulgida*); gayfeather (*Liatris* spp.); ornamental maiden grass (*Miscanthus sinensis*); Russian sage (*Perovskia* spp.); foxglove (*Digitalis grandiflora*); hardy geranium (*Geranium* spp.)

Shrub: arborvitae (*Thuja occidentalis*)

Bed in yard: daylily (*Hemerocallis* spp.)

BUTTERFLY GARDEN
Back bed by house: Joe Pye weed (*Eupatorium maculatum*); ornamental maiden grass (*Miscanthus sinensis*); butterfly bush (*Buddleia davidii*); purple coneflower (*Echinacea purpurea*); butterfly weed (*Asclepias tuberosa*); blue mist spirea (*Caryopteris* x *clandonensis*)

Front bed by yard: bee balm (*Monarda didyma*); catmint (*Nepeta* x *faassenii*); garden zinnia (*Zinnia elegans*); gayfeather (*Liatris* spp.); creeping phlox (*Phlox stolonifera*); sedum (*Sedum spectabile*)

BACKYARD SHADE GARDEN
Trees: birch (*Betula papyrifera*); redbud (*Cercis canadensis*); arborvitae (*Thuja occidentalis*); white oak (*Quercus alba*)

Shrubs: arborvitae (*Thuja occidentalis*)

Front bed by yard: hostas (*Hosta* spp.); coralbells (*Heuchera* spp.)

Center bed: lady fern (*Athyrium felix-femina*); bleeding heart (*Dicentra spectabilis*); astilbe (*Astilbe* spp.); lungwort (*Pulmonaria officinalis*); toad lily, (*Trycirtis hirta*)

Back bed: astilbe (*Astilbe* spp.); lady fern (*Athyrium felix-femina*); autumn fern (*Dryopteris ery-brosora*); Solomon's seal (*Polygonatum odoratum*); hosta (*Hosta* spp.);

heartleaf brunnera (*Brunnera macrophylla*); foamflower (*Tiarella cordifolia*); lenten rose (*Helleborus orientalis*)

ENCYCLOPEDIA OF EASY PERENNIALS

Perennials are highly versatile plants. Some are herbaceous, others are evergreen. And each plant has particular requirements for sun, soil, and water. However, if you know what individual perennials need in order to thrive, they will provide you with years of enjoyment.

The following perennials are listed alphabetically by their most common name. Other names are then sometimes listed, and each plant's botanical name and vital information follows. Play close attention to each entry's important zone information. For instance, if a plant is listed under Zone 5, it means that the area designated by the United States Department of Agriculture as Zone 5 (see pages 34–35), is the coldest area that this particular plant is considered hardy. That is, in Zone 5 chances are good that it will survive the winter, but it won't survive in Zone 4 and farther north. Also included under each entry is a detailed description of the plant, its easy-care growing requirements, propagation techniques, suggested uses, and related varieties and species.

This encyclopedia covers some of the easiest—and most popular—perennials. All of these plants should be readily available through your local garden center, or by mail-order. As you read through the following entries, let your imagination flow as you learn how each perennial will grow. Before you know it, your perennial garden will take shape!

Virginia bluebells

Hybrid Anemone, Autumn-flowering Anemone

Anemone species

Autumn-flowering anemones are a wonderful addition to the late summer garden because they bloom when color from other perennials is in short supply.

ZONE: USDA 5.

DESCRIPTION: The strong-stemmed, showy flowers are usually white or shades of pink with numerous golden stamens and very attractive compound leaves. Mature clumps can reach a height of 5 feet.

EASY-CARE GROWING: These plants are not difficult to grow but do need fertile, moist soil with plenty of organic matter mixed in. The roots (or rhizomes) will rot in heavy clay and wet earth. Fall-blooming anemones enjoy full sun in northern gardens but will adjust to partial shade. In the South, they need partial shade. In areas that have severe winters with little snow cover, plants should be mulched in late fall. *Anemone* x *hybrida* can be short-lived but it usually self-seeds and new plants emerge in the general vicinity of the original plants.

PROPAGATION: By division in early spring or by root cuttings in winter when the plants are dormant.

USES: Anemones are especially beautiful when grown in large clumps. They are also effective when allowed to self-seed and "wander" through the garden.

RELATED SPECIES AND VARIETIES: A number of *A.* x *hybrida* varieties are found including 'Alba' with white flowers; 'Honorine Jobert' with white flowers and showy yellow stamens; and 'Queen Charlotte' with pink semi-double flowers. *Anemone tomentosa* (also sold as *A. vitifolia*) is similar, but the pink-blossomed plants are hardier and more tolerant of both sun and drier soil. The foliage stays dark green and handsome from spring through frost. It is usually sold as 'Robustissima' and blooms a month earlier than *Anemone* x *hybrida*. *Anemone huphensis* is shorter than most at 2 to 3 feet tall; 'September Charm' produces single rose-pink flowers.

ASTER, MICHAELMAS DAISY
Aster species

The genus name of the asters is the Greek word for "star," and if ever a group of plants deserved such a bright appellation, this is the one.

ZONE: USDA 4.

DESCRIPTION: Daisylike flowers, usually about 1 inch wide with yellow centers, are carried on stiff, branched stems with long, narrow leaves. Bushy plants vary from 6 inches to 6 feet high, blooming from late summer into fall.

EASY-CARE GROWING: These plants do not need any pampering other than good soil drainage and full sun. Plant where they receive afternoon shade in the South. They grow well in average garden soil. New England and New York asters are prone to powdery mildew, so leave enough space between plants that air can circulate freely. Although asters in the field tolerate dry soil, those in the garden will need water during periods of drought. Moist soil reduces the severity of powdery mildew and keeps plants looking their best. Plants should be divided every two years when the center of the clump becomes bare or begins to look tattered. Plants can be pinched to produce neater clumps of flowers, or be left alone. Pinching after mid-July will delay flowering. Sometimes the taller types require staking.

PROPAGATION: By division in spring. Seedlings of many species can be variable both in growth habit and bloom, but adventurous gardeners might enjoy the challenge.

USES: Originally the English took the American New York field aster, *Aster novi-belgii*, and the New England aster, *A. novae-angliae*, and produced the Michaelmas daisy through hybridizing. Today the resulting varieties are stalwarts of the late summer and fall garden. The smaller types can be used as edgings for borders; the middle-sized asters are beautiful when grouped according to color; and the largest asters develop into effective backdrops to other plants. *Aster ericoides* (the heath aster), *A. novi-belgii*, and *A. novae-angliae* are

 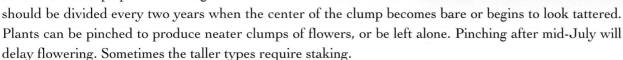

excellent cut flowers. Asters mix well with ornamental grasses—also blooming in the fall—and late-blooming perennial sunflowers (*Helianthus* species), sneezeweeds (*Helenium* species), and goldenrod (*Solidago* species).

RELATED SPECIES AND VARIETIES: The alpine aster, *Aster alpinus*, is a dwarf species with gray-green leaves and yellow-centered, purple-blue flowers, from 1 to 1½ inches wide. They are excellent in the rock garden or in the front of a border, blooming in summer. There are a number of colored forms available. The wild asters, *Aster novae-angliae* and *A. novi-belgii*, the parents of the Michaelmas daisies, are usually too rangy for the formal garden but they are excellent in the wild garden. Some good descendents from the original *Aster novae-angliae* line are 'Alma Potschke,' which grows to 3 feet tall, bearing bright rose flowers that bloom for almost six weeks; 'Harrington's Pink,' featuring pure pink flowers on 4-foot stems; and 'Purple Dome' with deep blue flowers on 18- to 24-inch plants. For shorter plants, look for *Aster novi-belgii* (also sold as *Aster* x *dumosus*) cultivars such as 'Alert,' which sports red flowers on 15-inch plants; 'Pink Bouquet,' with pink flowers on 14-inch plants; and 'Professor Kippenburg,' with lavender-blue, semi-double flowers on 12-inch plants. 'Rosenwitchel' grows 15 inches tall and is covered with lavender-pink flowers. 'Wood's Purple' and 'Wood's Pink' both grow 8 to 12 inches tall. The white wood aster, *Aster divaricatus*, is shade-tolerant. The Tatarian daisy, *Aster tataricus*, is hardy to USDA Zone 4 and produces light blue flowers on 6- or 7-foot-tall plants that do not need staking.

ASTILBE, GARDEN SPIREA
Astilbe species

Beautiful flowering plants for the shade garden, the astilbes available to gardeners today are usually the result of hybridizing, and listed as *Astilbe* x *arendsii* in garden books and nursery catalogs.

ZONE: USDA 4.

DESCRIPTION: Astilbes are lovely plants both for their dark green, fernlike foliage growing on polished stems and their long spikes of flowers that resemble feathery plumes. You can select from early, mid-, and late season blooming types.

EASY-CARE GROWING: Astilbes can be grown in full sun in cool northern regions but are best with partial shade, especially in the southern parts of the United States. Soil should be rich, slightly acidic, moist, and have plenty of organic matter mixed in. Divide the clumps every third year.

PROPAGATION: By division.

USES: Astilbe should be set out in groups of three or more. They mix well with hosta and ferns. Colors include white, pink, red, rose, and lilac. Heights vary from 12 to 40 inches. The white forms are especially effective against a shrub border or a line of bushes. They also make an effective ground cover. Astilbes turn a lovely shade of brown in the fall, and the dried flower heads persist until beaten down by heavy snow. They can be used as cut flowers in the summer and then dried for winter floral arrangements.

RELATED VARIETIES: 'Bridal Veil' bears white flowers on 2-foot stems; 'Peach Blossom' has salmon-pink flowers on 26-inch stems; pink 'Erica' blooms on 30-inch stems; and 'Montgomery' is a clear red on 28-inch stems.

RELATED SPECIES: *Astilbe chinensis* 'Pumila' spreads to make a good ground cover. The flowers are mauve-pink on 8- to 12-inch stems—perfect along the edge of a border and in the rock garden because they can tolerate drier soil than other types. *Astilbe tacquetii* 'Superba' bears large plumes of rose-pink flowers resembling cotton candy on 4-foot stems.

BABY'S BREATH
Gypsophila paniculata

Almost everyone has given or received a bouquet of flowers from the florist that contained a few sprays of baby's breath. The genus is Latin for the phrase "friendship with gypsum," because one species, *Gypsophila repens*, has been found growing on gypsum rocks.

ZONE: USDA 3.

DESCRIPTION: They feature small, blue-green leaves and a profusion of many-branched white-flowering panicles. Plants bloom in June and July.

EASY-CARE GROWING: Baby's breath require full sun and a deep, well-drained garden soil rich with humus. Even though the plants have taproots, they still require liberal amounts of water. If the soil is acidic—even a little—a cup of ground lime-stone per square yard should be added into the soil surrounding these lime-loving plants. Tall plants will probably require staking. They will rebloom if spent flowers are removed.

PROPAGATION: By seed. Propagation by cuttings requires patience, skill, and luck.

USES: Baby's breath are wonderful for filling in gaps in a bed or border. They are especially lovely when tumbling over rock walls or falling out of a raised bed.

RELATED VARIETIES: Two popular varieties are 'Bristol Fairy,' with pure white, double flowers, which grows to a height of 4 feet; and 'Pink Fairy,' which reaches 18 inches in height with pink doubles.

RELATED SPECIES: *Gypsophila repens* is a creeping baby's breath that grows 6 inches high, but covers an area to a width of 3 feet. 'Alba' is white; 'Rosea' is pink.

BALLOON FLOWER
Platycodon grandiflorus

A one-species genus, balloon flowers are so named because the unopened flowers look like small, rounded, hot-air blimps. The genus is named for the Greek word for "broad bell" and refers to the flower shape in full bloom.

ZONE: USDA 4.

DESCRIPTION: Balloon flowers are clump-forming perennials with alternate, light green leaves on stems usually between 1½ and 3 feet tall. The balloon-shaped buds open into bell-shaped flowers that are 2 to 3 inches wide. The sap is milky.

EASY-CARE GROWING: Balloon flowers like moist, well-drained soil in full sun. In the South, they should be planted where they will receive afternoon shade. It is not until late spring that the first signs of life appear, so be careful not to dig out or damage slow-to-emerge plants during spring garden cleanup. Flower stems usually need staking. Individual dead flowers should be removed with sharp pruning scissors to prolong bloom. Be careful not to damage the new flower buds developing behind the old flowers. Balloon flower has a deep taproot and is very long-lived.

PROPAGATION: By division in mid-spring or seed.

USES: Balloon flowers bloom during most of the summer and are attractive in borders. Smaller types grow best along garden edges. They are especially effective when used in conjunction with white pansies, the white obedient plant, or bright yellow yarrow.

RELATED VARIETIES: 'Albus' bears white flowers and 'Hakona Blue' has two layers of petals—both varieties bloom on 16-inch stems. 'Mariesii' has blue flowers on 12- to 16-inch stems, 'Sentimental Blue' is 6 to 9 inches tall with blue flowers, and 'Shell Pink' bears larger soft-pink blooms on 2-foot stems and is best when grown in some shade.

BASKET-OF-GOLD
Aurinia saxatilis

Originally included in the Alyssum genus, these charming flowers of spring have now been moved to an older genus that is named after a chemical dyestuff used to stain paper. Basket-of-gold belongs to the mustard family.

ZONE: USDA 3.

DESCRIPTION: Attractive low, gray foliage growing in dense mats gives rise to clusters of golden-yellow, four-petaled flowers floating 6 to 12 inches above the plants.

EASY-CARE GROWING: Aurinia needs very well-drained soil in full sun. Plants will easily rot in damp locations and they resent high humidity. Plants should be sheared back by one-half after blooming. The foliage is evergreen, so plants should not be cut back in the fall or winter. Cut back damaged foliage in the spring after you see new growth emerging. Aurinia can be short-lived in the South.

PROPAGATION: Divide in the fall.

USES: Aurinias are quite happy growing in the spaces between stone walks, carpeting the rock garden, or growing in pockets in stone walls where their flowers become tumbling falls of gold.

RELATED VARIETIES: 'Citrina' bears lemon-yellow flowers and grows 12 to 15 inches tall; 'Flore Plena' has double, yellow blooms; and 'Compacta' has a denser habit of growth.

RELATED SPECIES: *Alyssum montanum*, 'Mountain Gold,' grows 4 inches tall and has silvery, evergreen leaves and fragrant, bright yellow flowers. It makes a dense ground cover.

BEARD TONGUE
Penstemon barbatus

There are so many kinds of penstemons that the American Penstemon Society actually publishes a newsletter and illustrated guides for choosing these plants. Except for one species from Asia, the rest are native to North America, with most coming from the West Coast. *Penstemon barbatus* is one of the easiest species to grow in the eastern United States because it is quite winter-hardy and heat-tolerant.

ZONE: USDA 2.

DESCRIPTION: Basal foliage is evergreen in warmer climates. The leaves are sometimes whorled. Flowers are tubular in airy, terminal clusters atop strong stems, blooming from spring into summer.

EASY-CARE GROWING: Penstemons come from areas with rough growing conditions and should never be planted in soil that stays wet or damp. A thin, rocky soil in full sun is best.

PROPAGATION: By division in spring, or seed.

USES: Penstemons are exceedingly attractive in the garden and have a long season of bloom. Plants look best set out in groups so that a mass of flowers is in view. Some gardeners succumb to their beauty and are inspired to create entire specialty gardens out of this genus. They are excellent as cut flowers.

RELATED VARIETIES: 'Alba' has white flowers; 'Elfin Pink' has clear pink flowers on 1-foot–high branches, making it perfect for the front of the border; 'Prairie Fire' is a vivid orange-red on 22-inch stems; 'Prairie Dusk' has purple flowers on 20-inch stems.

RELATED SPECIES: *Penstemon digitalis* 'Husker Red' has maroon leaves through spring and summer and wiry stems with pretty white flowers. It tolerates wetter soil conditions than other species.

Bee Balm, Bergamot, Oswego-Tea
Monarda didyma

These are stunning, native American plants that have been garden favorites for decades. They are closely related to culinary mint and all have aromatic foliage. Bee balm flowers produce a lot of nectar, so they are very attractive to hummingbirds, butterflies, and bees.

ZONE: USDA 3.

DESCRIPTION: Sturdy, square stems growing as tall as 4 feet have simple leaves. They are topped with crowns that are studded with lipped flowers blooming from summer into fall.

EASY-CARE GROWING: They grow along stream banks in the wild and grow best in a slightly moist spot and full sun. They can become floppy when grown in the shade. Extra water during dry periods is needed.

The plants spread by underground stems, so excess plants should be dug and removed from time to time. Deadhead spent flowers for extended bloom. Bee balm is prone to mildew if plants are crowded or the soil doesn't stay moist. Clumps tend to die out in the center and should be divided every two or three years to keep them healthy.

PROPAGATION: By division in early spring, or seed.

USES: Useful for the wild garden in moist soil or by the waterside, bee balm is also beautiful in beds or borders because of its long season of bright bloom.

RELATED VARIETIES: The following varieties have good levels of mildew resistance: 'Blue Stocking' is not really blue, but a brilliant, deep violet; 'Jacob Cline' has deep red flowers; and 'Marshall's Delight' bears rich pink flowers.

RELATED SPECIES: The flowers of *Monarda fistulosa* or wild bergamot are light lavender or whitish pink and are not as brilliant as *M. didyma*. However, *M. fistulosa* is very mildew resistant and recent breeding work is improving its flower color. 'Claire Grace' is a new mildew-resistant variety with soft lavender flowers that tolerates drier soil.

BELLFLOWER

Campanula species

The botanical name is from the Latin word for "bell" and refers to the shape of the flowers. The genus includes annual flowers, biennials, and perennials suitable for formal and wild gardens. They range in height from low-growing rock garden types to 5 feet.

ZONE: USDA 4.

DESCRIPTION: Although bellflowers are usually various shades of blue, many are available in white. Flowers bloom from late spring into early summer. Basal leaves are usually broader than the stem leaves and form rosettes or mats.

EASY-CARE GROWING: Bellflowers need a good, moist, but well-drained soil with plenty of organic matter mixed in. In the North, plants will tolerate full sun as long as the soil is not dry. Elsewhere, a spot in semi-shade is preferred. Most bellflowers flower best if they are deadheaded regularly.

PROPAGATION: By division, cuttings, or seed.

USES: According to the species, plants are beautiful in the border, useful in the rock garden, and fine for the shade or wild garden.

RELATED SPECIES AND VARIETIES: *Campanula carpatica* blooms at a height of 10 inches with solitary blue flowers. It is effective as an edging, or tumbling over a small rock cliff. Mulch to keep the roots cool. 'Blue Clips' and 'White Clips' have excellent compact form and 3-inch flowers. 'Joan Elliott' has many 1- to 3-foot-tall stems of violet-blue flowers. 'Superba' has large clusters of violet flowers and tolerates heat well. 'Chettle Charm' has silvery-white flowers with lavender margins. 'Grandiflora Alba' bears large, white flowers; 'Blue Gardenia' has double, blue blossoms; and 'Telham Beauty' is 3 to 4 feet tall with larger-than-usual China-blue flowers. *Campanula poscharskyana*, or Serbian bellflower, is a ground creeper with star-shaped, 1-inch blossoms of lavender-blue, perfect for the partially shaded, dry rock garden or in a hanging basket. Sheer it back to basal foliage after it finishes flowering. *Campanula rotundifolia* is known as harebell, or bluebells of Scotland. It is very cold tolerant and looks best when grown in mountain or northern regions. Excellent drainage is essential.

BETHLEHEM SAGE, LUNGWORT
Pulmonaria species

One of the first flowers of spring, the lungworts are exceptional plants for the quality of both their blossoms and foliage. The leaves are dotted with white or silver and provide a bright spot in the shaded garden.

ZONE: USDA 3.

DESCRIPTION: Lungworts have simple, basal leaves growing to 1 foot long, which are spotted with silver-white splotches. Leaves do not grow as long in warmer, drier growing regions. Terminal clusters of flowers, which in many species open as pink and then turn to blue, bloom in the spring. Flowers often bloom before the leaves fully develop.

EASY-CARE GROWING: While lungworts will persist in poor soil, they are truly lovely when planted in good, moist garden soil, in partial to full shade. Water must be provided during times of drought. However, they do not like standing water and will rot in winter if the soil stays wet. If foliage is disfigured by powdery

mildew or gets ragged looking in the summer, cut it back. Keep the soil moist and fresh and new foliage will emerge.

PROPAGATION: By division in fall.

USES: Lungworts are lovely plants for the shade garden. They look great in front of large hostas or mixed with purple-leaved coralbells.

RELATED SPECIES AND VARIETIES: *Pulmonaria longifolia* has long, narrow leaves. 'Bertram Anderson' has electric violet-blue flowers and silver-spotted leaves. *Pulmonaria saccharata*, or the Bethlehem sage, has leaves that are three times as long as they are broad. The old reliable cultivar 'Mrs. Moon,' has large silver leaf spotting; 'Roy Anderson' is heat-tolerant—good for planting in the South—with light blue flowers and small, silver spots on the leaves. 'Sissinghurst White' bears large white flowers.

BISHOP'S HAT, BARRENWORT
Epimedium species

Distinctive foliage and delicate flowers make epimediums a wonderful addition to any garden. They grow naturally in bright woodlands with light shade.

ZONE: USDA 5.

DESCRIPTION: Epimediums have sturdy, heart-shaped leaves with a toothed edge on wiry stems that closely resemble a jester's hat or, in some species, a bishop's miter or biretta. They bloom in April and May.

EASY-CARE GROWING: Epimediums like open shade, although they will tolerate some sun. They appreciate good drainage and humus-rich soil. They grow well under tree canopies and easily coexist with tree roots. Epimediums are slow to establish but do spread gradually. Cut old foliage off in early spring before the new growth begins.

PROPAGATION: By division in late spring after flowering is finished.

USES: Classified by most nurseries as a ground cover, epimediums are also excellent for the edge of a border. Some of the species are evergreen where the climate allows. They mix well with hostas and are a good choice to plant under Japanese maples or large shade trees.

RELATED SPECIES AND VARIETIES: *Epimedium grandiflora* grows about 1 foot high with white flowers tinged with pink at the tips of the spurs. 'Rose Queen' has crimson leaves and rose-pink flowers. *Epimedium* x *rubrum* has red leaves when young, and pale red flowers on 12-inch stems. It is the best species for a fast-growing ground cover. *Epimedium* x *versicolor* 'Sulphureum' produces the densest foliage and bears yellow flowers on 10-inch stems. *Epimedium* x *youngianum* 'Niveum' has white flowers on 8-inch stems; 'Roseum' bears lilac flowers.

BLACKBERRY LILY, LEOPARD FLOWER
Belamcanda chinensis

Belamcanda is a genus of irislike plants that are native to China, Japan, and Korea. It has escaped from gardens and is now established in pastures and along roadsides in many northeastern states.

ZONE: USDA 5.

DESCRIPTION: Blackberry lily has 2- to 3-foot-long, sword-shaped leaves that give rise to tall flower stems. Each stem holds many 2-inch orange flowers speckled with red. Flowers only last for a day, drying with a twist into tight spirals, then falling as seed pods develop. They are, however, soon followed by other blossoms throughout July and August. Eventually the oval, green seed pods split open to reveal attractive, shiny black seeds that resemble blackberries.

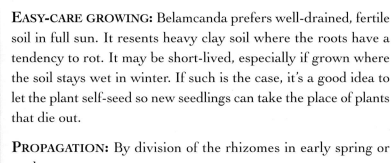

EASY-CARE GROWING: Belamcanda prefers well-drained, fertile soil in full sun. It resents heavy clay soil where the roots have a tendency to rot. It may be short-lived, especially if grown where the soil stays wet in winter. If such is the case, it's a good idea to let the plant self-seed so new seedlings can take the place of plants that die out.

PROPAGATION: By division of the rhizomes in early spring or seed.

USES: A large grouping of these plants looks especially attractive when backed by a stone wall or when planted among mounds of ornamental grasses.

RELATED VARIETY: 'Freckle Face' produces light orange flowers that bloom the first year if planted early.

RELATED SPECIES: *Belamcanda flabellata* has 8-inch leaves and bears yellow flowers. 'Hello Yellow' grows to 15 inches and is a great addition to the summer garden.

BLANKET FLOWER
Gaillardia x *grandiflora*

These popular perennials bear cheerful and bright daisylike flowers. Gaillardias are easy to grow and bloom for many weeks. They are named after Gaillard de Clarentonneau, a French botanist.

ZONE: USDA 3.

DESCRIPTION: This particular species is a vigorous hybrid of two native types. Slightly hairy leaves are usually basal; 3- to 4-inch flowers have purple centers (disk flowers) and notched petals (ray flowers) in a number of bright colors. They bloom throughout the summer.

EASY-CARE GROWING: Blanket flowers need full sun and well-drained garden soil. They do not grow well in rich soil. Sometimes short-lived, the plants will not survive winter in wet soil. Each year, the center of the crown dies back and new plants appear off center. They are easily transplanted to bloom that summer. They bloom over a long period even if spent blossoms are not removed.

PROPAGATION: By division in early spring or seed.

USES: Gaillardias work well in the front of a border, particularly if grouped in threes or fives. They also provide marvelous cut flowers. The dwarf varieties are fine as edging plants.

RELATED VARIETIES: There are a number of varieties available with new types showing up every year. 'Baby Cole' is a dwarf selection—6 to 8 inches tall—with yellow flowers banded in red. 'Goblin' reaches a 12-inch height and bears red flowers with yellow borders. The 'Monarch Strain' features reds, yellows, and browns.

BLEEDING HEART
Dicentra spectabilis

These heart-shaped pendant flowers with spurs at the base (the genus name means "two-spurred") have attractive foliage until they go dormant in midsummer.

ZONE: USDA 2.

DESCRIPTION: Bleeding heart has clusters of rose, pink, or white flowers on arching sprays and bluish, fernlike foliage. It grows 18 to 36 inches wide and 18 inches tall. It is one of the earliest perennials to flower in the shaded garden.

EASY-CARE GROWING: Bleeding hearts need open or partial shade and evenly moist, slightly acidic soil containing plenty of humus. Plenty of compost should be added when planting; mulch around bleeding heart with pine needles or pine bark to provide a bit of acidity.

PROPAGATION: Divide dormant rhizomes after plants have flowered or take 3-inch-long root cuttings in March.

USES: This plant is a lovely sight when planted next to a moss-covered log with ferns in the background or between the gnarled roots of a large tree.

RELATED VARIETIES: 'Alba' has white flowers.

RELATED SPECIES: *Dicentra eximia*, or the fringed bleeding heart, has fernlike blue-green foliage. It begins flowering later than *D. spectabilis*, but the plant does not go dormant in summer heat. In fact, it flowers most of the summer—if protected from the sun and given ample moisture. It grows 18 inches tall. *Dicentra formosa* is a rose-colored species found from British Columbia to California and usually grows about 18 inches high. It is more drought-tolerant than *D. eximia* and does not do well in wet, humid weather. 'Luxuriant' is a hybrid that will bloom throughout the summer, especially if old flowers are removed.

BLUEBEARD, BLUE MIST SPIREA
Caryopteris x clandonensis

Blue mist spirea is technically a woody shrub. However, it loses leaves in the winter and usually dies back to the ground every year, so it is often treated as a perennial. It mixes very well with other sun-loving perennials and is great for fall flower color.

ZONE: USDA 5.

DESCRIPTION: Opposite leaves are 3 inches long and narrow. The undersides are grayish-white. Blue-purple flowers are formed toward the top of each stem in late summer or early fall. Plants grow 3 to 4 feet tall and 4 feet wide.

EASY-CARE GROWING: Full sun and well-drained soil are best for this perennial. It does not need rich soil or extra moisture. Blue mist spirea is frequently used in water-conserving landscapes in western states. Do not cut back stems in the fall or winter. Wait until you see new growth emerge in the spring, then cut back just above that. Plants spread by way of underground runners.

PROPAGATION: Take stem cuttings in spring or early summer.

USES: Incorporate this perennial as you would a small shrub. Blue mist spirea can be planted singly or in groups of three. It mixes well with yellow flowers that bloom at the same time of the year, such as orange coneflower and goldenrod. It blooms at the same time that monarch butterflies migrate and butterflies find it an irresistible nectar source.

RELATED VARIETIES: 'Blue Mist' has gray-green leaves and light blue flowers. 'Heavenly Blue' has dark green leaves and deep blue flowers. 'Longwood Blue' has silvery foliage and sky blue flowers.

BLUE STAR FLOWER, WILLOW AMSONIA

Amsonia tabernaemontana

Bluestars are native wildflowers found in the wild from New Jersey to Tennessee, west to Kansas, and south to Texas.

ZONE: USDA 3.

DESCRIPTION: Plants bloom in clusters of lovely pale blue flowers in May and June. After flowering has passed, the upright stems with narrow leaves are still attractive. In the fall, the foliage turns a beautiful butterscotch-yellow.

EASY-CARE GROWING: Plants can be established in any reasonably fertile garden soil. They grow between 2 and 3 feet tall and are somewhat tolerant of dry soil, remaining shorter when located in such situations. Full sun or light shade and supplemental moisture during dry periods is ideal. If grown in shade, blue star may need a circular support frame to keep foliage from flopping. Plants can also be cut back by one-third to one-half after flowering, to control height and prevent plants from flopping. It self-sows, with seedlings becoming bushy clumps in a few years.

PROPAGATION: By seed, division, or stem cuttings in the early spring.

USES: Bluestars belong in any wild garden and in perennial beds or borders. They are especially attractive mixed with wild or garden columbines (*Aquilegia* spp.) and planted in the vicinity of tree peonies.

RELATED SPECIES: *Amsonia hubrectii*, Arkansas amsonia, can be grown in USDA Zone 6 and warmer. The flowers are lighter blue. In fall, the golden-yellow foliage is spectacular. A species called *salicifolia* is native to the southeast United States and bears very narrow, long leaves.

BOLTONIA
Boltonia asteroides

oltonias are American native wildflowers found in poor or damp soil as far north as Manitoba, Canada, south to Florida, and west to Texas.

ZONE: USDA 4.

DESCRIPTION: Plants resemble asters with sturdy stems, narrow leaves, and dozens of white flowers in clusters. Blooming from late summer into fall, a well-situated boltonia will be covered with bloom.

EASY-CARE GROWING: Boltonia prefers well-drained, moist, organic soil and full sun. It will tolerate periods of drought and can be grown in light shade if you are willing to stake it. Divide every four to five years to control spread.

PROPAGATION: By division in spring.

USES: Since boltonia grows 5 feet high, it is best at the rear of the garden. A line of these plants will become a flowering hedge of great charm. They can be used with ornamental grasses or mixed with fall asters, goldenrod, Joe Pye weed, Russian sage, and sedum 'Autumn Joy.'

RELATED VARIETIES: 'Nana' is a new dwarf cultivar that has pinkish-lilac flowers and only grows 28 inches tall. 'Pink Beauty' has soft pink flowers and grows 4 to 5 feet tall. Its growth habit is somewhat open and lanky and it generally needs staking. 'Snowbank' has white flowers and grows 3 to 4 feet tall. It does not require staking if grown in full sun. It can also be cut back by one-half to two-thirds in early June to produce a fuller plant that doesn't need support.

HEARTLEAF BRUNNERA

Brunnera macrophylla

Originally from western Siberia, the flowers of these plants look similar to forget-me-nots. They are named after Swiss botanist Samuel Brunner.

ZONE: USDA 3.

DESCRIPTION: Showy blue flowers about one quarter-inch wide bloom in clusters during spring. In the spring, leaves are light green and small. After plants stop flowering, the heart-shaped leaves become much larger (up to 6 inches across) and form mounds of attractive foliage. Plants get 12 to 18 inches wide and 20 inches tall if they are grown in the right conditions.

EASY-CARE GROWING: Brunnera prefers a deep, moist soil with plenty of organic matter and shade. It will tolerate a fair amount of sun in northern gardens if given plenty of moisture. It grows very well around shaded stream banks and other water features.

PROPAGATION: By seed, root cuttings in winter when the plants are dormant, or division (it can be divided every six to ten years).

USES: Brunnera is lovely in the front of a border or when mixed with hosta and ferns. It is exceptionally attractive when naturalized at the front edge of a wooded area or in a wild garden along a stream or near a pool. After blooming, the large leaves make an effective ground cover.

RELATED VARIETIES: 'Hadspen Cream' is variegated with an irregular, creamy white margin. It is somewhat difficult to grow. 'Langtrees' has green leaves with a ring of silver spots near the edge and tolerates drier conditions.

BUGLEWEED
Ajuga species

Bugleweed is excellent both for the color of its leaves as well as its attractive flowers. Three species are commonly available.

ZONE: USDA 3.

DESCRIPTION: Plants grow along the ground. The flat, rounded leaves form mats that keep weeds at bay. They bloom in spring with irregular flowers in spiked clusters.

EASY-CARE GROWING: Bugleweed is easy to grow in ordinary, well-drained garden soil that gets partial shade. It tolerates sun but looks better in shade. As a ground cover, plants should be placed 10 inches apart; they will soon fill in. They are evergreen in areas with mild winters or that get good snow cover.

PROPAGATION: By division in spring or fall.

USES: Bugleweed is an excellent ground cover. It is also beautiful when used as edging at the front of a border. In a rock garden, it is perfect for tumbling over rock edges. Although it grows quickly, plants are easily uprooted.

RELATED SPECIES AND VARIETIES: *Ajuga genevensis*, or Geneva bugle weed, grows faster than *A. pyramidalis* but doesn't spread as vigorously as *A. reptans*. It also tolerates more sun than the other two species if given plenty of water. It needs winter protection in Zone 4. *Ajuga pyramidalis*, or upright bugleweed, bears brilliant blue flowers on 6-inch spikes, hovering above deep green leaves. It stays bushy, not spreading as widely as others in the clan. 'Metallica Crispa' has purplish-brown leaves with crisped edges and 'Alba' bears white flowers. *Ajuga reptans* is the ground cover of note. Be aware that it can be invasive if it escapes the garden and gets into the lawn. 'Burgundy Glow' bears blue flowers with leaves in three colors; new growth is burgundy-red, but as the leaves age, they become creamy white and dark pink. It is not particularly long-lived. 'Catlin's Giant' has 8-inch-long blue flower spikes and bronze-green foliage.

Butterfly Bush, Summer Lilac

Buddleia davidii

Like blue mist spirea, butterfly bush is really a woody shrub. However, it loses its leaves and dies back to the ground every year. It is commonly sold as an herbaceous perennial.

ZONE: USDA 5.

DESCRIPTION: Butterfly bush grows into a large arching shrub and is covered with 4- to 10-inch-long wands of flowers (usually purple) from June or July until the first frost. The foliage is gray-green or dark green on top and silvery gray on the bottom side. Plants can grow from 5 to 10 feet tall—the size depends on the cultivar grown.

EASY-CARE GROWING: Grow in well-drained, fertile soil and full sun. Prune back in spring after you see new growth emerging at the base of the plant in spring. Deadhead frequently for the heaviest bloom and largest flowers. With the exception of an occasional winter kill, butterfly bush is a very durable, trouble-free plant.

PROPAGATION: By seed or stem cuttings collected between June and August.

USES: Incorporate as you would a small shrub. Butterfly bush can be planted singly or you can scatter several throughout a large garden. It mixes well with flowers that bloom at the same time as it does, as well as with ornamental grasses. It is a fabulous nectar source for butterflies all summer.

RELATED VARIETIES: 'Black Knight' has dark purple flowers and is a vigorous grower. 'Lochinch' is larger than most and will grow 12 feet tall. It has 12-inch-long clusters of purple flowers with orange centers and is fragrant. 'Nanho Blue' and 'Nanho Purple' are smaller plants that grow 3 to 5 feet tall. 'Pink Delight' has fragrant deep pink flowers. 'Royal Red' is the best red variety with purple-red flowers on spikes up to 20 inches long.

BUTTERFLY WEED, MILKWEED

Asclepias tuberosa

Butterfly weed is a native American wildflower that is not only at home in the wild garden but contributes to the perennial border as well. Like all members of the milkweed family, it has milky sap in the stems and inflated seed pods with silky seeds that float on air currents.

ZONE: USDA 4.

DESCRIPTION: Bloom time is late spring through summer. In northern zones, plants often come up late in the season. Flowering plants resemble a dish full of orange candy on 2-foot stems. The individual flowers are striking in their beauty. The plants bear thin leaves and are most attractive when in flower. They grow 2 to 3 feet tall and 2 feet wide. As with many wildflowers, plants are smaller if grown in lean, dry soil.

EASY-CARE GROWING: These are easy plants to grow and they tolerate a wide variety of soil types—surviving in the thinnest of poor soils but generally doing their best in an average garden setting with full sun and good drainage. Once a butterfly weed develops a good root system, it is a very drought-resistant plant. However, immature plants must be watered until mature, especially during prolonged dry spells. Butterfly weed is slow to emerge from the ground in the spring so be careful not to damage it during spring garden clean-up.

PROPAGATION: By seed or division in early spring.

USES: Butterfly weed does well in meadows and wild gardens and is essential in a garden designed to attract butterflies. The flowers can be cut for fresh bouquets. The seed pods are also used in dried arrangements. All members of the milkweed family are host plants for monarch butterflies and their young.

RELATED SPECIES: The swamp milkweed, *Asclepias incarnata*, has pinkish flowers on 2- to 4-foot stems and grows well in wet situations.

CANDYTUFT
Iberis sempervirens

Many species of candytuft originally came from Iberia—the ancient name of Spain—hence the genus of Iberis. They bloom profusely in the spring.

ZONE: USDA 3.

DESCRIPTION: Candytuft is a many-branched, small, evergreen shrub with smooth, oblong leaves about 1½ inches long. In the spring, it bears flat-topped clusters of white flowers, sometimes flushed with pink. It can grow as tall as 10 inches and spreads about 20 inches wide.

EASY-CARE GROWING: Candytuft needs a good, well-drained garden soil in a sunny spot. The leaves are usually evergreen, but in most areas of Zone 3 and 4, winter causes severe damage to the leaves. Mulch is necessary if snow cover is lacking. Cut off dead branches in the spring to stimulate new growth. Cut plants back by half after spring flowering to eliminate seed development and to keep growth looking fresh and healthy. Plants quickly become dense mats after cutting back.

PROPAGATION: By seed or separating plants that form along rooted stems as they spread out from the center of the plant.

USES: Candytuft is great for a rock garden where it can tumble around and over rocks. It is also excellent as edging in a border and is well suited to growing in pots.

RELATED VARIETIES: 'Alexander's White' is a good cultivar that grows 10 to 12 inches tall and flowers heavily. 'Autumn Snow' stays about 10 inches high and blooms both in spring and fall. 'Little Gem' is a dwarf at a height of 6 inches. 'Pygmea' is a prostrate form that forms a low mat close to the ground. It has small flowers in the spring.

CARDINAL FLOWER
Lobelia cardinalis

ardinal flowers are native American wildflowers of great beauty. They grow naturally in the eastern half of the United States.

ZONE: USDA 2.

DESCRIPTION: Basal foliage, evergreen in mild climates, and oblong leaves on stout stems produce 2- to 4-foot spikes of truly brilliant red flowers that can be seen in the summer over a great distance because of the intense color. Up to 50 flowers are produced on a single 2-foot-long flower spike. Flowers open at the bottom of the spike first and then proceed to open upward to the tip. They flower for about three weeks in late summer. Cardinal flowers are often found growing at the edge of stream banks in the open shade of tall trees.

EASY-CARE GROWING: Cardinal flower grows best in light shade and humus-rich, moist soil. Plants grown in dry soil languish. Remove flower stalks after blooming, but let a few seed pods form so new plants replace the usually short-lived parents. Cardinal flower will be killed in the winter if not properly protected with a light winter mulch in areas without adequate snowfall. Apply the mulch after the ground freezes. Be sure to remove the mulch in early spring as soon as the soil warms. Divide the plants every two or three years by removing the new plants that develop alongside parent plants.

PROPAGATION: By division or seed.

USES: Cardinal flowers are unexcelled for waterside planting. They are also stunning in beds, borders, and wild gardens with moist soil. Hummingbirds and butterflies love this plant and visit the flowers frequently for nectar.

RELATED SPECIES: *Lobelia siphilitica*, great blue lobelia, has smaller blue flowers on stout, 1- to 3-foot-long stems. It blooms from late summer into fall.

CATMINT, FAASSEN NEPETA
Nepeta x faassenii

Catmint is a showy, fragrant member of the mint family but it is not the legendary plant favored by cats. That plant is another member of the mint family, catnip or *Nepeta cataria*.

ZONE: USDA 4.

DESCRIPTION: Catmint generally grows 12 to 18 inches tall and 18 inches wide. Many spikes of light blue to violet-blue flowers are held out over mounds of silvery-gray foliage.

EASY-CARE GROWING: In much of the country, catmint grows best in full sun and well-drained soil. It will grow in partial shade in regions warmer than Zone 5 and needs afternoon shade in the South. Many varieties will bloom again in the fall if you sheer them back by half or two-thirds after the first flush of flowers fades and dies in spring.

PROPAGATION: By division in spring, or stem cuttings.

USES: Low-growing varieties make good edging plants and look terrific in front of shrub roses. Groups of three or more plants are most effective.

RELATED VARIETIES: 'Blue Wonder' grows into a 12- to 15-inch-tall compact mound. It flowers for several weeks in spring and will flower again in the fall if you cut it back after the spring bloom. 'Six Hill's Giant' grows 24 to 36 inches tall and bears 10-inch-long, dark violet flower spikes. The foliage is greener than other types. 'Walker's Low' grows 12 inches tall and has soft lavender blue flowers from spring through fall.

CHRYSANTHEMUM
Dendranthema x grandiflorum (D. x morifolium, Chrysanthemum x morifolium)

Fall-flowering garden mums provide a burst of color late in the season just as many gardens start to flag. They have been bred over hundreds of years resulting in a great variety of form and color.

ZONE: USDA 5.

DESCRIPTION: Leaves are usually divided and often aromatic. Stems are strong and flowers are showy.

EASY-CARE GROWING: Chrysanthemums need good, well-drained soil in full sun. They will die if grown in heavy, clay soil. Most have shallow roots, so the soil should be evenly moist through the growing season. Garden mums are heavy feeders and should be fertilized two or three times during the growing season. They benefit from frequent pinching, which promotes bushy growth and more flowers. Mums that have wintered over can be pinched when plants are 6 inches tall, then again every three weeks. Mums planted in the spring should be pinched for the first time two or three weeks after planting. Divide plants in the spring every two years to maintain strong growth and good flowering.

PROPAGATION: By stem cuttings, division, or seed.

USES: Chrysanthemums are perennial in some gardens but are usually best treated as annuals. In the fall, potted mums can be purchased from garden centers and transplanted around the garden where they will continue to bloom until severe frost cuts them down. Garden mums can be used in masses in front of ornamental grasses or to fill in areas where annuals have peaked and need to be replaced. They also do well in containers.

RELATED VARIETIES: Hundreds of cultivars are available. Selections should be made based on personal preference and recommendations by your local garden center retailer. Northern gardeners should look for the 'Minn' series of garden mums which flower before frost.

RELATED SPECIES: *Dendranthema weyrichii* — or *Chrysanthemum weyrichii* — is a fairly recent Japanese import that flowers in very late fall with 2-inch single flowers with a yellow eye. *D. zawadskii* var. *latilobum* (also sold as *D. x rubellum*) 'Clara Curtis' grows 18 to 24 inches tall with single pink flowers and yellow centers.

COLUMBINE
Aquilegia species

Columbines are beloved by hummingbirds, are perfect for cut flowers, and have a very long season of bloom. The genus is from the Latin word for "eagle."

ZONE: USDA 3.

DESCRIPTION: The leaves are compound with rounded lobes. Columbine blooms in spring and early summer and many flower colors are available. Flowers may be of all one color or may be two-toned.

EASY-CARE GROWING: Columbines are easy to grow, adapting to almost any reasonably fertile garden soil—although they must have good drainage. They will do well in full sun or partial shade, especially in the South. Flowering can be extended by removing all of the spent blossoms before plants go to seed. Plants are often short-lived but you can encourage the development of new seedlings by leaving a few seed pods on the plant. Hybrid columbine will not produce seedlings that look like the parent.

PROPAGATION: By seed.

USES: Columbine flowers are attractive and long-blooming and the foliage texture contrasts nicely with bolder plants. They are also good additions to a lightly shaded woodland garden.

RELATED VARIETIES: Among the best are the McKana hybrids, with 2-foot-tall plants bearing blossoms of blue, pink, maroon, purple, red, and white. The Music hybrids are 20-inch plants with flowers of intense yellow, blue and white, red and white, and pure white. 'Dragonfly' has flowers with longer-than-average spurs.

RELATED SPECIES: *Aquilegia caerulea*, the Colorado columbine, has sky-blue blossoms with white centers on wiry stems growing to 2 feet. *Aquilegia canadensis* is the wild Eastern columbine. Its graceful flowers have long, red spurs and yellow faces on 1- to 2-foot stems. It is one of the easiest wildflowers to cultivate. *Aquilegia flabellata* is excellent in the rock garden or as an edging for a border. 'Nana Alba' has pure white flowers and remarkable blue-green foliage.

PURPLE CONEFLOWER
Echinacea purpurea

This stalwart American native was once found naturally from Ohio to Iowa and south to Louisiana and Georgia. They can still be seen growing wild in prairies and meadows and along roadsides.

ZONE: USDA 5.

DESCRIPTION: Cone-shaped, prickly heads of a bronze-brown are surrounded by rose-purple petals on stout stalks from 2 to 4 feet high. Leaves are alternate, simple, and coarse to the touch.

EASY-CARE GROWING: Coneflowers will take almost any well-drained garden soil in full sun. They grow well in partial shade in warmer regions. If soil is too rich, the flowers frequently need to be staked. Spent flowers should be removed to prolong blooming. Plants can be divided in spring to reduce their spread, if necessary.

PROPAGATION: By division in spring or seed.

USES: Coneflowers are beautiful plants for the back of a small garden border and they are a welcome addition to a wildflower garden. They are especially striking when mixed with orange coneflowers (*Rudbeckia* spp.) and ornamental grasses. They make excellent cut flowers, provide nectar for butterflies, and seed for birds.

RELATED VARIETIES: 'Bright Star' bears maroon flowers and 'Magnus' has rosy purple petals with a dark disk. 'Kim's Knee High' is a new introduction that grows 15 to 20 inches tall and bears bright pink flowers. 'White Swan' has white flowers.

RELATED SPECIES: *Echinacea pallida* is a similar wildflower species from the Midwest with thinner and more graceful pink petals.

CORALBELL, ALUMROOT
Heuchera species

Coralbells are American wildflowers that originally came from the southern states of New Mexico and Arizona and the country of Mexico. Recent breeding work on types with colored foliage has rocketed these plants to a place of prominence in the shade garden.

ZONE: USDA 4.

DESCRIPTION: Coralbells have mounds of basal leaves that are rounded and lobed, rising from a thick rootstock. Many varieties have ornately colored or patterned leaves. Plants are usually evergreen. The flowers resemble tiny bells on 1- to 2-foot wiry stems blooming from spring into summer.

EASY-CARE GROWING: In areas with hot summers, these plants need shade. In cooler regions they can be grown in full sun or in areas that receive afternoon shade. Coralbells should be planted in good, well-drained garden soil with a high humus content, and kept somewhat moist during the growing season. In winter, coralbells will die if the soil stays wet. Old foliage should be pruned off in spring to make way for fresh growth. Every three years they must be divided to prevent overcrowding. Spent flowers should be removed.

PROPAGATION: By division in spring.

USES: Coralbells are an exciting addition to the perennial border or a rock garden. Dark-leaved types are stunning in combination with hosta and with perennials with gold leaves. They are also good cut flowers.

RELATED VARIETIES: 'Bressingham Bronze' has crinkled, bronze-purple leaves. 'Chocolate Ruffles' has large chocolate-brown leaves with purple undersides. 'Stormy Seas' has undulating leaves with silver, lavender, and pewter markings. 'Mount St. Helens' has smaller green leaves and tall stems of cardinal red flowers.

COREOPSIS
Coreopsis species

Over 100 species of coreopsis exist. Most of the commonly used varieties are very long bloomers and are some of the easiest perennials to care for.

ZONE: USDA 5.

DESCRIPTION: Small daisies in various shades of yellow and orange grow on wiry stems. Some species only grow 8 inches tall and others can reach 30 inches. Leaves vary from simple, oval shapes in basal rosettes to foliage that is decidedly fernlike. Tickseed coreopsis, *C. grandiflora*, with relatively wide leaves, and thread-leaf coreopsis, *C. verticillata*, with much thinner leaves, are the two species most gardeners are familiar with.

EASY-CARE GROWING: Coreopsis are happy in almost any well-drained garden soil in full sun. They are drought resistant and an outstanding choice for hot, difficult places. Cut plants back after they bloom to encourage repeat bloom.

PROPAGATION: By division in spring or seed.

USES: Excellent for the wild garden and in the formal border, these flowers are prized for cutting. The smaller types are also good for edging plants. Threadleaf coreopsis is suitable for patio containers.

RELATED SPECIES AND VARIETIES: *Coreopsis grandiflora* and *Coreopsis lanceolata* are freely interchanged. *C. grandiflora* 'Sunray' bears double, golden-yellow flowers on 2-foot stems. *C. lanceolata* 'Goldfink' has golden-yellow flowers on 9-inch stems. 'Brown Eyes' has a ring of dark brown close to the center of golden flowers on 20-inch stems. *Coreopsis verticillata* bears bright yellow flowers on 2-foot mounds of foliage. 'Moonbeam' has creamy light yellow flowers. 'Golden Gain' is a long-blooming type bearing dozens of bright yellow flowers on 16- to 18-inch stems; 'Zagreb' is similar with bright yellow flowers on 18-inch stems. *Coreopsis auriculata* 'Nana' is a dwarf form that stays about 1 foot tall and bears orange flowers.

DAISY, SHASTA DAISY

Leucanthemum x *superbum* (*Chrysanthemum* x *superbum*)

Long-blooming Shasta daisies have been a popular mainstay of the summer garden for many years and are a quintessential cut flower.

ZONE: USDA 5.

DESCRIPTION: White flowers with yellow centers are 2 to 3 inches in diameter. The leaves are dark green and toothed. Varieties range from 8 to 36 inches tall. Single- and double-flowered forms are available.

EASY-CARE GROWING: Shasta daisies are not fussy. Good drainage is essential. Plants will not survive the winter in wet soil. They grow and flower best in full sun. Daisies are shallow-rooted plants, so keep them well watered during dry periods. They benefit from a light spring fertilization and a mid-summer boost of quick-acting liquid foliar feed. Keep plants deadheaded for maximum flower production. Plants bloom vigorously and then become weak or die out the following season. Sometimes the center of the plant becomes woody with just a few tufts of fresh growth in the spring. Replace old plants with new ones either by allowing plants to self-sow, by dividing and replanting, or by purchasing new plants every two years. Most Shasta daisies self-sow so you can allow seedlings to develop to replace declining plants.

PROPAGATION: By division or seed.

USES: Medium to tall varieties provide the garden with a light, airy texture as flower stems sway in the breeze. Shorter types are effective at the front of a perennial planting. All types are good nectar sources for butterflies and make excellent cut flowers.

RELATED VARIETIES: 'Alaska' is a proven performer. White flowers with yellow centers are 3 inches across and are borne on 2- to 3-foot stems. 'Becky' shows great heat tolerance in the South. Large white flowers on 36-inch stems stand upright without support.

RELATED SPECIES: The Nippon daisy, *Nipponanthemum nipponicum* (*Chrysanthemum nipponicum*), bears 2- to 3-inch white flowers on 3-foot woody stems. The leaves are thick and scalloped. The foliage is very aromatic. Nippon daisies are excellent in seaside gardens. *Tanacetum parthenium* (*Chrysanthemum parthenium*), or feverfew, is an old medicinal herb. Bushy plants grow to 3 feet with aromatic leaves.

DAYLILY
Hemerocallis species

The scientific name of the wild daylily is *Hemerocallis fulva*—hemero means "beautiful" and callis "day" in Greek. Each individual blossom opens, matures, and withers in 24 hours or less. Daylilies were originally brought over the trade routes from China to England. Then settlers coming to America from Europe brought these hardy plants to brighten their colonial gardens. Almost every home had tawny daylilies and a clump of lemon lilies. Today there are over 30,000 varieties in existence

ZONE: USDA 3.

DESCRIPTION: Daylilies have tuberous and fleshy roots with mostly basal, sword-shaped leaves. The leaves usually grow up to 2 feet long with tall, multi-branched stalks, each containing many 6-petaled lily-like flowers. Once blooming only in summer, new varieties—called rebloomers—begin to bloom in May and continue blooming into September.

EASY-CARE GROWING: Daylilies are literally carefree. They need only good, well-drained soil in full sun. They benefit from afternoon shade or partial shade in the South.

PROPAGATION: By division in spring or fall.

USES: Entire gardens can be created using these marvelous plants, or they can be interspersed with other perennials. By mixing early, mid-, and late season blooming types, daylilies can bloom from late spring to fall.

RELATED VARIETIES: There are hundreds, if not thousands, of daylily varieties available every year from nurseries. Let your personal preference guide you in selection.

RELATED SPECIES: *Hemerocallis citrina* blooms in summer with arching, 3-foot leaves and fragrant, yellow blossoms on 4-foot stems that open in the early evening and last to the following day. *Hemerocallis fulva* is the tawny orange daylily, too rough for today's perennial bed or border, but still excellent for a ground cover, or for a wild or meadow garden. *Hemerocallis lilio-asphodelus* is the old-fashioned lemon lily with fragrant flowers in late May and June.

DELPHINIUM, LARKSPUR
Delphinium species

Although some types of delphinium are more difficult to grow than other perennials, they are usually worth the extra effort because they are such stately plants.

ZONES: USDA 4 to 6.

DESCRIPTION: The alternate leaves are cut and divided. Plants produce tall spikes of showy flowers, usually in shades of blue, each having a long spur behind the petals.

EASY-CARE GROWING: They need full sun in mild climates, and afternoon shade where summer temperatures are intense. Soil should be fertile, deep, well-drained, evenly moist, and high in organic matter. If the soil is too acidic, lime should be added. Delphiniums are greedy feeders and must be supplied with compost or well-rotted manure. In addition, they benefit from feedings of a 5-10-5 fertilizer every year. Without protection, staking is often required. After flowering, flower heads should be removed unless seeds are wanted. Delphiniums are short-lived perennials that lose their vitality after two or three years. Since they grow easily from seeds and cuttings, propagation is never a problem.

PROPAGATION: By cuttings, careful division, or seed.

USES: Short types can be used in the front of a garden, the Belladonna hybrids in the middle, and the taller types at the back.

RELATED SPECIES: *Delphinium* x *belladonna*, Belladonna hybrids, grow 3 to 4 feet tall and have branched flower stalks instead of a single spike. If spent flowers are removed, they will usually bloom all summer. *Delphinium elatum*, or the hybrid bee delphinium, reaches 6 feet, with flowers available in white, lavender, blue, and purple. *Delphinium grandiflorum* is a charming shorter species that grows 3 feet tall or less. It is short-lived and best treated as an annual. The Pacific hybrids produce 6-foot stalks that must be staked even when given protection from wind; the flowers in various shades of blue and pink are spectacular. The Connecticut Yankee series is a bush form that grows well in the South. A newer group called the Mid-Century Hybrids grow 4 to 5 feet tall with strong stems and good mildew resistance.

DIANTHUS, PINK, CARNATION
Dianthus species

Pinks are hardy flowers that grow in the garden and carnations are the greenhouse-grown flower worn as a boutonniere or used in a florist's bouquet—although the terms are often mixed. There are at least six garden-worthy dianthus species and many choice varieties.

ZONE: USDA 3.

DESCRIPTION: These largely short-lived perennials have narrow leaves that, depending on the species, are either green or blue-green. Five-petaled flowers with fringed edges often have a distinct, spicy-sweet scent.

EASY-CARE GROWING: Plants need full sun and good, well-drained garden soil that is slightly alkaline. Pinks grown in hot, humid climates need midday shade. They do not tolerate wet soil. Plants supplied with 1 inch of water through the growing season and minimal water in the winter are the most likely to be persistent. Many species benefit from division every two years.

PROPAGATION: By stem cuttings, division, or seed.

USES: Pinks are excellent choices for a rock garden, hanging over the edges of a wall, or for the front of a garden, especially as edging plants. They make wonderful cut flowers and many will bloom all summer if spent flowers are deadheaded.

RELATED SPECIES AND VARIETIES: *Dianthus* x *allwoodii* have bluish-green foliage with flowers of red, pink, or white—often with darker centers—that reach a height of 18 inches. *Dianthus barbatus*, or sweet william, produces clusters of multi-colored flowers and is lovely in the border of a garden. Sweet william is a biennial, but self-seeding produces new flowering plants year after year. *Dianthus deltoides*, or the maiden pink, forms low mats of leaves usually covered with delightful, single flowers on 6- to 12-inch stems and is perfect for the rock garden. It needs good drainage. 'Brilliant' bears bright, double crimson flowers. *Dianthus gratianopolitanus*, or the cheddar pink, produces clouds of flowers on 6- to 8-inch stems and is right at home in the rock garden. The flowers are about 1 inch wide and are beloved by butterflies. 'Bath's Pink' bears hundreds of soft pink flowers for many weeks.

FALSE INDIGO, WILD INDIGO
Baptisia australis

A beautiful plant in leaf and flower—and after going to seed—false indigo was originally planted to produce a blue dye for early American colonists. Unfortunately, the dye wasn't fast. The name of the genus is from the Greek word for "dipping," which is also the root word for baptism.

ZONE: USDA 3.

DESCRIPTION: This large plant grows to 3 to 4 feet in height. The blue-green, compound leaves on stout stems are attractive all summer, and the dark blue, pea-like flowers are 10 to 12 inches long. The seed pods that develop eventually turn black and are quite showy.

EASY-CARE GROWING: Baptisia grows readily in well-drained soil in full sun, but will also grow in poor soil. The white form tolerates some shade. The root systems of older plants become so extensive that they are difficult to move.

PROPAGATION: By division or seed.

USES: In time, a single baptisia plant will cover an area several feet in diameter with gracefully arching foliage. Because they die down to the ground in winter, a line of these plants makes a perfect deciduous hedge when plants are spaced 3 feet apart. A single plant can be used as a fine focal point in the border. In addition, these plants are excellent for a meadow or wild garden, or planted along the edge of the woods. The flowers are also beautiful when cut. After the first frost, the leaves, as well as the inflated seed pods—often called Indian rattles—turn black.

RELATED SPECIES: The prairie false indigo, *Baptisia alba*, has 12- to 20-inch-long racemes with white flowers. Unlike some of the other species, *B. alba*'s foliage remains attractive in the fall. It grows 2 to 3 feet tall and will tolerate some shade. *Baptisia leucantha* (*B. lactea*) is very similar to *B. alba*. The main difference is in fruit size and shape.

FERNS

Many different species of hardy ferns are easy to grow in shaded gardens with moist soil. Some types even grow from rock crevices and in fairly sunny locations. The foliage of different species is either coolly elegant or lushly textured and wild looking. Ferns are a tough group of garden plants.

DESCRIPTION: Ferns have two basic growth habits: clump-forming or creeping. The fronds, or leaves, of clumpers grow in an upright vase-shaped cluster. Clump-forming types spread more slowly than creeping types. Creepers send out underground rhizomes and spread rapidly.

EASY-CARE GROWING: Ferns grow best in soil that is high in organic matter and slightly acidic. In the wild, ferns grow through thick layers of leaves that fall from overhead trees. Ferns in the garden also appreciate a layer of leaf litter as well as an additional 4 to 6 inches of humus-rich organic matter tilled into the soil. Most ferns like constant moisture, although they can stand short dry periods.

PROPAGATION: By division.

USES: Ferns can be used in formal or informal designs. Clump-forming types can be used as single accent plants or in combination with shade-loving shrubs or perennials such as hosta, brunnera, and coralbells. Creeping forms can be planted in large masses as a ground cover. Ferns look great around streams, ponds, or water features.

RELATED SPECIES: The autumn fern, *Dryopteris erythrosora*, is an evergreen clump-forming fern that grows 12 to 24 inches tall. New fronds sport coppery-pink tips. It grows easily through USDA Zone 5 in shade or partial shade. The Christmas fern, *Polystichum acrostichoides*, is an evergreen fern with leathery, dark green fronds that grow 1 to 2 feet tall into an upright, formal-looking clump. Protected from winter wind. It is hardy to USDA Zone 4. Lady fern, *Athyrium felix-femina*, is a deciduous fern and one of the easiest to grow through USDA Zone 4. Lacy fronds are bright green and graceful. Dense clumps are 2 feet tall. Shade to partial shade is best. The ostrich fern, *Matteucia struthiopteris*, spreads to form large patches. Deciduous fronds are dark green and triangular, growing 3 to 4 feet tall up to USDA Zone 2. The Japanese painted fern, *Athyrium nipponicum* 'Pictum,' will thrive through USDA Zone 3. Arching fronds grow 12 inches tall and are olive green with a metallic-gray and red sheen.

FORGET-ME-NOT
Myosotis sylvatica

There are over 50 species of forget-me-nots and none of them are very long-lived. However, most self-sow and bloom every year from new seedlings.

ZONE: USDA 3.

DESCRIPTION: The fragrant blossoms are a brilliant true blue with small yellow centers. The airy flowers open in April and May. Forget-me-not usually blooms sporadically throughout the summer in northern gardens. *Myosotis sylvatica* is a biennial. However, abundant self-seeding assures that plants will appear and bloom every spring. Leaves are 2 to 3 inches long and hairy. Forget-me-nots grow 6 to 8 inches tall.

EASY-CARE GROWING: Plant in dappled shade or where plants receive morning sun and afternoon shade. They will grow in full sun if the soil is rich and moist. They are easy to grow, needing at least 4 inches of well-drained, reasonably fertile garden soil. In the South, thin dense leaves in June in order to open up plants and to reduce the occurrence of leaf rot.

PROPAGATION: By division or seed.

USES: These plants are quite beautiful in large clumps or in a border. They are the perfect plant to mix with spring-blooming bulbs and columbine.

RELATED VARIETIES: 'Royal Blue Compact' grows 6 to 8 inches tall in compact, bushy mounds. 'Victoria Blue' is an early flowering variety. 'Victoria Rose' is an early variety with pink flowers.

FOXGLOVE, YELLOW FOXGLOVE
Digitalis grandiflora

Most foxgloves are biennial plants, but *Digitalis grandiflora* (still called *D. ambigua* in some catalogs) is a long-lived perennial for the garden. The common name alludes to the belief that a fox could become invisible and make off with the chickens if wearing this plant's blossoms on its paws.

ZONE: USDA 3.

DESCRIPTION: Yellow foxgloves are strong-stemmed plants with simple alternate leaves. Their yellow, nodding, bell-like flowers usually line up on one side of the stem and bloom in summer. Unlike some of the other foxgloves, yellow foxglove foliage looks good all season.

EASY-CARE GROWING: Yellow foxgloves want a moist, well-drained garden soil in partial shade. If dead flower stalks are removed, plants sometimes bloom a second time.

PROPAGATION: By division or seed.

USES: Yellow foxglove looks good in the perennial garden when planted in groups of three or more. It is superb in the wild garden and among plants that have naturalized along the edge of a wooded area. They are also lovely in front of a line of shrubbery or small trees.

RELATED SPECIES: *Digitalis lutea* is a perennial that grows 2 to 3 feet high and bears many small, creamy yellow flowers on one side of each blooming stalk during May and June. *Digitalis purpurea* is the common foxglove. It is a stately plant that can grow 3 to 4 feet tall with lavender flowers. Plants need constant moisture and semi-shade. The foliage is tattered and worn by late summer. It is a biennial, so it must reseed or new plants must be planted every year. Seedlings take two years to flower.

Gas Plant, Burning Bush
Dictamnus albus

There is only one species in this genus, and rumor has it that its leaves, if lighted with a match on a breathless summer evening, will produce a gas and burn with a faint glow. Many have tried, but few have reported success.

ZONE: USDA 4.

DESCRIPTION: A handsome, carefree plant resembling a small bush, gas plant grows between 2 and 3 feet high with glossy, compound leaves that have a faint lemony scent. In June and July, white or purple flowers are borne on long spikes.

EASY-CARE GROWING: Plants are slow to establish, but once rooted in, they will persist for decades. Choose the location for a gas plant with care because the roots resent any disturbance. A spot in full sun with humus-rich, moist, well-drained soil is needed. Gas plant needs cool night temperatures to look its best. Plants are usually purchased as 2-year-old seedlings and take another two years to get established in the garden. Allow 3 feet between plants if grouped.

PROPAGATION: By seed.

USES: In flower or out, this is an attractive plant for the border. Even after flowering has passed, the seed heads provide visual interest. Flowers are good for cutting.

RELATED VARIETIES: 'Albiflorus' has white flowers and 'Purpureus' bears soft mauve flowers.

GAURA
Gaura lindheimeri

There are a number of gauras that are native American wildflowers. However, this particular species is the best for the garden and is well adapted to many areas of the country. Found naturally in the southern states of Louisiana and Texas and farther south to Mexico, this perennial's white flowers slowly fade to pink as they age.

ZONE: USDA 5.

DESCRIPTION: Gaura has alternate, lance-shaped leaves up to 3 inches long on stout stems. The stems are wispy and reddish in color. The white 1-inch, 4-petaled flowers slowly turn pink as they age. Flowers open at the bottom of the spike first and continue opening toward the tip. Flowering stems can reach as high as 3 or 4 feet. If flowers are deadheaded, gaura blooms from late spring until fall. In northern climates, they don't start blooming until late in the season.

EASY-CARE GROWING: Gauras need full sun in deep, well-drained garden soil, as the taproot is very long. They are drought- and heat-resistant and grow very well in arid western gardens and hot, humid southern gardens.

PROPAGATION: By seed or division in spring.

USES: Perfect for both a dry garden and a wild garden, they are also very attractive in a formal border and are charming when planted with asters and ornamental grasses.

RELATED VARIES: 'Whirling Butterflies' has sterile flowers that are bright white. Stems are reddish and the foliage is willowy. Plants grow to 30 inches tall. 'Siskiyou Pink' has brilliant reddish-pink flowers with white stamens. It only grows 18 inches tall.

GAYFEATHER, BLAZINGSTAR
Liatris species

Gayfeather is native to North America and makes a very good garden plant. They are especially valuable since they bloom in late summer or fall when the bed or border can use a punch of color. Plant several different species to maximize the blooming season because each one flowers at a different time.

ZONE: USDA 3.

DESCRIPTION: Simple, linear leaves on usually stout stems grow in clumps from thick rootstocks. Flower heads are set along tall spikes and bear fluffy disk flowers, resembling feathery staffs. Unlike most other spiked flowers, gayfeather flowers open from the top down. They bloom in late summer or early fall.

EASY-CARE GROWING: Gayfeather grows easily in full sun. Most species are well adapted to dry, rocky soil although they are quite happy in slightly richer soil as long as it is well drained. Wet soil in winter will usually kill the plants. *Liatris spicata* requires moister soil than other species. The taller varieties sometimes require staking, especially if grown in rich soil.

PROPAGATION: By seed or division of older plants in spring.

USES: Clumps of liatris are perfect for the bed and border. Mix them with white garden phlox, ornamental grasses, golden lace flower, and orange coneflower. Butterflies love the nectar and they are especially good cut flowers.

RELATED SPECIES: *Liatris aspera*, rough blazing star, is the latest flowering species with purple flowers, which are attractive to monarch butterflies. *Liatris microcephela* is short, growing 18 to 24 inches tall. It bears multiple flowering stems in midsummer and is only hardy to USDA Zone 6. *Liatris scariosa*, or the Eastern blazing star, bears intense purple flowers on spikes from 3 to 6 feet tall in August and September. *Liatris spicata* 'Kobold' bears rose-purple flowers on 2- to 3-foot stems in early summer.

HARDY GERANIUM, CRANESBILL
Geranium species

The female part of this flower resembles the shape of a crane's beak. These plants are not to be confused with the common summer annual or florist's geranium that is really a *Pelargonium*.

ZONES: USDA 3 to 5.

DESCRIPTION: These usually low-growing plants have lobed or deeply cut leaves on forked stems and bear 5-petaled flowers in great profusion from spring to summer.

EASY-CARE GROWING: Growing requirements vary by species. Generally, moist soil and full sun to partial shade are fine. Late afternoon shade is usually beneficial in the South. There are a few species that grow well in heavy shade. Most should be divided every 3 years to keep foliage fresh and to encourage flowering.

PROPAGATION: By division, root and stem cuttings, or seed.

USES: In a border or a rock garden, cranesbills are lovely plants. They make an excellent ground cover and are striking when grown along a wall. Hardy geraniums look good at the front of the border and can be used to hide bare stems of taller, leggy plants.

RELATED SPECIES AND VARIETIES: *Geranium* x *cantabrigiense*, or Cambridge geranium, grows 6 to 8 inches tall with light green leaves and purple-violet flowers. It forms a thick mound of foliage. 'Biokova' has white flowers tinged with rosy pink and grows 10 to 12 inches tall. 'Biokova Karmina' has raspberry-red flowers. *Geranium dalmaticum* grows 6 inches high with rose-colored flowers. It spreads by rhizomes. In the fall, leaves turn red-orange. Plant in full sun in well-drained soil. 'Album' is a white-flowered form. *Geranium endressii* 'Wargrave Pink' has salmon-pink flowers held above shiny green leaves. Plant in full sun in the North but provide afternoon shade in the South. Good drainage is essential for longevity. *Geranium* x 'Johnson's Blue' has bright, blue-violet flowers that bear dozens of blossoms in June and July. It grows 15 to 18 inches tall. *Geranium macrorrhizum*, bigroot geranium, is an excellent ground cover and one of the easiest geraniums to grow. Plant in full sun or partial shade in the South.

Geum, Avens
Geum species

There are over 50 species of geums and all are members of the rose family. They produce brilliant flowers and have attractive leaves coated with silky down. Many produce interesting, fluffy seed heads. Most of the garden forms are hybrids of two or more species.

ZONES: USDA 3 to 4.

DESCRIPTION: Geums produce clumps of lobed, shiny green leaves covered with silky down on hairy stems. The plants grow to 2 feet tall and bear single flowers that are about 1½ inches across. Flower colors are red, yellow, or white. They bloom strongly in spring and continue intermittently in summer if they are deadheaded.

EASY-CARE GROWING: Geums are easily grown where summers are cool. They need well-drained, moist soil with plenty of humus. Keep roots cool with a layer of mulch. In Northern regions, plants can be grown in full sun. In warmer areas, afternoon shade helps keep them cooler. Divide plants every two years to keep them in peak flowering condition. In areas subject to subzero temperatures without snow cover, these plants should be mulched.

PROPAGATION: By seed or division in spring.

USES: Geums are attractive in the front of a border and in a rock garden where the bright flowers are very showy.

RELATED VARIETIES: 'Mrs. Bradshaw' is a double, brilliant scarlet and 'Lady Stratheden' is a warm yellow.

GOAT'S BEARD
Aruncus dioicus

Goat's beard is a North American native of great beauty. A healthy, established plant is an impressive sight when it flowers.

ZONE: USDA 3.

DESCRIPTION: Plants can grow between 4 and 6 feet tall and have a bushlike form. The compound leaves are light green and look similar to astilbe foliage. Plants come into bloom in late spring or early summer and produce several showy plumes that consist of hundreds of tiny, creamy-white flowers. The plants are dioecious (meaning that male and female flowers grow on separate plants), but there is little difference between them, and most nurseries never mark the distinction. In autumn, the leaves turn a nice yellow.

EASY-CARE GROWING: Goat's beard is easy to grow as long as it gets light shade and moist soil. It can be grown in more sun in the North if it receives ample moisture. Goat's beard does very well in moist bottom-land. If it lacks for water in the summer, the foliage turns brown and crisp. Cut off damaged leaves and keep the soil moist to promote new growth.

PROPAGATION: By seed or division in the spring (division is very difficult with older plants).

USES: Because it wants light shade rather than deep shadow, goat's beard is a fine choice for areas under groups of high trees. It looks great as a background for a group of hosta. A waterside planting is also a good choice.

RELATED VARIETIES: 'Kneiffi' is the cut-leaf goat's beard, reaching a height of 4 feet with leaves that are cut into narrow segments.

RELATED SPECIES: *Aruncus aethusifolius* is a dwarf variety from Korea that makes a 6- to 8-inch mound of feathery leaves and short but showy spires of white flowers. It is a charming edging plant for the garden border.

GOLDEN LACE, SCABIOUS PATRINIA
Patrinia scabiosifolia

Patrinia is an underused, easy-to-grow perennial that mixes well with almost any other type of plant. It deserves a spot in a sunny garden.

ZONE: USDA 5.

DESCRIPTION: Hundreds of airy yellow flowers are held in large, flat-topped inflorescences above the leaves. Plants flower from summer through fall on two-year-old plants. Plants grow between 36 and 60 inches tall, depending on which form you get. The Korean form grows 60 to 72 inches tall while the Japanese form (usually sold as the variety 'Nagoya') grows 36 inches tall.

EASY-CARE GROWING: Patrinia is very heat tolerant and should be planted in full sun in well-drained, moist soil. Cut flowering stems down at the base before seed sets to keep foliage looking fresh, but leave enough seed heads to ensure that a few seedlings get established. Patrinia is sometimes short-lived. If foliage looks rough at summer's end, cut it back and keep the soil moist to encourage fresh growth. Leave the basal foliage in place through the winter.

PROPAGATION: By seed.

USES: Patrinia looks great when used as a filler with other summer and fall bloomers. Try blending it with ornamental grasses, blue mist spirea, gayfeather, Joe Pye weed, purple cone-flower, and Russian sage. Patrinia makes an excellent cut flower.

GOLDENROD
Solidago hybrids

Goldenrods are quintessential fall perennials. However, these North American wildflowers have suffered from bad press due to the mistaken belief that they cause hay fever and the fact that they can become weedy when brought into the garden. Since most of the 130 or so species found in the wild cross-pollinate with ease, the plants described are unspecified hybrids.

ZONE: USDA 5.

DESCRIPTION: Goldenrods are strong-stemmed plants, often growing to 6 feet tall, with either smooth or lightly toothed alternate leaves arising from a root crown or rhizome. They bloom in late summer or fall with sprays of small, usually golden-yellow flowers.

EASY-CARE GROWING: Goldenrods are happy in full sun or partial shade with humus-rich, well-drained garden soil. They will also do well in moist conditions and along the edge of woodlands. Keep old flowers pruned off to reduce unwanted seedlings and to encourage longer bloom.

PROPAGATION: By seed, division in spring, or stem cuttings.

USES: Great for the wild garden, along a stream, or naturalized in meadow gardens, goldenrods are also striking in the open bed or border. Some of the less invasive types work well in large-scale plantings. They are excellent for cutting.

RELATED SPECIES AND VARIETIES: 'Crown of Rays' bears golden-yellow flowers on 24- to 36-inch stems. Plants are self-supporting and are not overly invasive. Use a shovel to remove plants around the outer perimeter if clumps get too large. 'Golden Thumb' is a good dwarf form. It grows 12 inches tall and has yellow-green foliage and yellow flowers. *Solidago rugosa* 'Fireworks' is a splendid plant growing 3 to 4 feet tall. It produces large, arching wands of golden-yellow flowers in the fall. *Solidago sphacelata* 'Golden Fleece' has many sprays of golden-yellow flowers on spreading stems. It grows 15 to 18 inches tall.

Goutweed, Bishop's Weed
Aegopodium podagraria

English gardeners can talk for hours about the evils of ground elder, or goutweed as it is called in the United States. The botanical name means "little goat feet," and sometimes the plants have a tendency to run through the garden, out of control, using roots that ramble like little running feet.

ZONE: USDA 2.

DESCRIPTION: Plants grow about 12 inches high with green leaves that are divided into three leaflets. The flowers are white, rangy, and not very attractive—they should be cut off to prevent self-seeding.

EASY-CARE GROWING: Goutweed adapts to just about any garden soil. Plants like partial shade, but they will grow in full sun if the soil is moist. If leaves turn brown from summer heat, they can be cut back and new fresh leaves will appear.

PROPAGATION: By division in spring or fall.

USES: This plant makes a fine ground cover or planting for a slope that is too steep either for grass or for a regular garden. Since each piece of root will eventually lead to a new plant, care should be taken in planting. Goutweed should not be mixed in with other perennials. Plants should be grown where a solid edging will stop their spread, such as in a strip between a building and a sidewalk. They can also be used as a ground cover under trees and shrubs. Goutweed also does well in containers.

RELATED VARIETIES: 'Variegata' is a plant with very attractive, light green leaves that are edged with white. It is much preferred over the solid green species.

ORNAMENTAL GRASSES
Gramineae family

Ornamental grasses are a distinct family of plants unexcelled for use in the perennial garden. The foliage is usually of primary interest and the flowers are secondary. Still, many of the seed heads are very beautiful and add interest in the fall and winter.

ZONE: USDA 5.

DESCRIPTION: The grass family (*Gramineae*) runs the gamut—from 120-foot giant bamboos to tiny, dwarf fescues only a few inches high. The stems, or culms, of the true grasses are usually round and hollow, and the stem sections are joined by solid joints, or nodes. Root systems are very fibrous, growing deep into the ground. Therefore, they hold up well during periods of drought. The leaves are parallel-veined and consist of a blade and a sheath. The flowers are usually feathery or plumelike.

EASY-CARE GROWING: Unless specified, grasses need a good, well-drained garden soil in full sun. A few will do equally well in moist or wet soil. The only chore connected with the perennial grasses is the annual pruning of the larger types in early spring. That is the time to cut the dead stems and leaves to within 6 inches of the ground before new growth begins. Division for the larger clumps is best accomplished with hearty digging and an ax to divide the roots.

PROPAGATION: By division in spring.

USES: The large grasses make superb specimen plants. Both their seed heads and leaves provide interest through fall and winter unless they are beaten down by winter snows. Ornamental grasses are great "anchors" in the garden when used behind shorter perennials. Some of the grasses can form valuable screens. Many types produce an astounding amount of flowers that can be used in dried or winter bouquets.

RELATED SPECIES AND VARIETIES: *Calamagrostis* x *acutiflora* 'Karl Foerster,' or feather reed grass, is a clump-forming, narrowly vertical plant. Leaves are deep green and lustrous and grow about 4 feet tall. Flowers grow to 6 feet tall and are loose purplish plumes. Although it prefers sun, this grass will grow in half-day shade and will tolerate heavy clay through USDA Zone 4. *Chasmanthium latifolium*, or sea oats, is a valuable ornamental grass that will do well in partial shade. It grows naturally on wooded slopes and along streams. It is a clump former that grows about 3 feet high. It is upright when grown in sun and somewhat arching when grown in shade. After the first frost, the leaves and flowers turn a rich, tannish-brown and remain on the plant well into December. If the dangling flowers are picked while still green, they will retain their color. Use through USDA Zone 5. *Imperata cylindrica* 'Red Baron,' or Japanese blood grass, has leaf blades from 1 to 2 feet high that begin the season green but quickly turn a deep, rich red. It spreads very slowly by underground rhizomes. This grass is happy in full sun or a bit of shade and prefers moist, fertile soil. It is fairly drought resistant once established. It is a good grass to use through USDA Zone 6. *Miscanthus sinensis* 'Morning Light,' or maiden grass, is one of the very best miscanthus varieties. It has thin, fine-textured leaves with a narrow white strip along the edge. It grows in clumps to 4 feet tall with a rounded, arching form and looks very elegant in the garden. Showy white flowers form in the fall. Grow in full sun and good soil through USDA Zone 5. *Miscanthus sinensis* 'Strictus,' or porcupine grass, has green leaves with yellow bands. It is a rather upright clump-former growing as high as 8 feet, and usually doesn't flop over. Flowers are reddish. Plant through USDA Zone 5. *Pennisetum alopecuroides*, or fountain grass, produces narrow leaves that grow like fountains. It is a clump-former, reaching about 3 feet high. Arching flower stalks end in dense floral cylinders that resemble foxtail grass flowers. They make good cut flowers. It is reliable to USDA Zone 6 although it often survives in colder climates.

HARDY HIBISCUS, ROSE MALLOW, SWAMP MALLOW

Hibiscus moscheutos

This native American plant is a real eye-catcher with 10-inch diameter flowers that are produced on large, vigorous plants.

ZONE: USDA 5.

DESCRIPTION: Flowers are similar to hollyhocks and grow up to 10 inches across. They bloom in pink, purple, red, or white with a dark red eye. Plants have alternate leaves, green above and white and hairy beneath, on stems up to 7 feet in height. Plants bloom most of the summer.

EASY-CARE GROWING: Mallows prefer moist garden soil in full sun. They grow best with consistent soil moisture but will adapt to drier soil after they are established. In time, all the members of the clan make big clumps up to 3 feet across, so allow plenty of room for growth. The mallows seem to be unaffected by salt, making them an excellent choice along highways. Without a snow cover, a mulch must be applied in cold areas.

PROPAGATION: By division or seed.

USES: Mallows are fine for wild gardens and in places with damp soil. They are also excellent large plants for the back of a bed or border. When planted in groups, the flowers will make the backyard look like a tropical paradise.

RELATED VARIETIES: 'Anne Arundel' has pink flowers and attractive, deeply cut leaves. 'Blue River II' has 10-inch, clear white flowers that are long bloomers. The leaves are slightly blue-green. 'Lord Baltimore' bears loads of ruffled, crimson-red flowers. 'Southern Belle' produces huge, 10-inch flowers in red, rose, pink, and white on 4-foot plants.

RELATED SPECIES: *Hibiscus coccineus* bears bright red flowers on 4-foot plants and is native to the southern United States. It is not hardy north of Philadelphia, Pennsylvania.

HOLLYHOCK
Alcea rosea

Hollyhocks are the quintessential cottage garden flower. Although they are short-lived biennials, hollyhocks are once again becoming popular in American gardens.

ZONE: USDA 3.

DESCRIPTION: Plants grow 6 feet tall and usually have a single, unbranched flowering stalk that bears a dozen flowers. Flowers are single or double and come in many colors.

EASY-CARE GROWING: Plant in full sun in average soil. Water and fertilize hollyhocks throughout the growing season for the best appearance and bloom. Scratch a balanced granular fertilizer into the soil around plants when new foliage is 2 inches high, then switch to a high-phosphorus, water-soluble formula such as 10-30-20 in June. Apply the water soluble formula to the tops and undersides of leaves twice a week. Tall varieties can be cut back once or twice to create shorter plants that don't need staking. Cut back by half in May and again in mid-June. Plants will be about half the normal height and will flower several weeks later. After plants have flowered, remove all old flowering stems and old foliage around the bases of the plants. If you want plants to reseed, leave a few ripe flower stalks for this purpose.

PROPAGATION: By seed.

USES: Plant at the back of the border and use shorter perennials to hide their bare lower stems.

RELATED VARIETIES: 'Indian Spring' is a mix of single flowers in white, yellow, rose, and pink. 'Powder Puffs' is a mix with 4-inch-wide fully double flowers in white, yellow, rose, and red.

HOSTA, PLANTAIN LILY
Hosta species

The backbone of the shade garden, hostas come in all sizes, forms, and colors—and there are hundreds of named varieties. Depending on the type you select and growing conditions, they can be grown in deep shade and full sun.

ZONE: USDA 3.

DESCRIPTION: Hostas are usually distinguished by large clumps of basal leaves with pronounced veining and smooth or wavy edges. Leaf colors come in various shades of green, yellow-green, gold, and blue-green. Many varieties have white, cream, or yellow variegation. Lilylike flowers on tall stems (or scapes) in white or shades of purple bloom in late summer. Some of the flowers are fragrant.

EASY-CARE GROWING: Hostas do best in good, well-drained, moist garden soil with plenty of humus. Depending on the species and variety they will grow in partial shade, moderately deep shade, or a good deal of sun. Some of the more durable types such as 'Royal Standard' adapt to dry shade. They dislike wet soil in winter. Once established, hostas can survive for generations.

PROPAGATION: By division.

USES: Hostas are indispensable in the shade garden and are often the primary plant used. The smaller types are excellent at the front of the border or as ground cover. The larger varieties become elegant specimen plants forming gigantic clumps of leaves over the years. Hostas are a natural choice to plant in a mixed shade border that includes shrubs and trees and other perennials. Although usually grown for the leaves, the flowers are often beautiful and can be used in cut flower arrangements. Hummingbirds sometimes visit the flowers for nectar.

RELATED SPECIES: Some hosta suppliers stock well over 200 different species and varieties of this adaptable plant. The following list is a sampling of a few of the good choices that are commonly available. They are grouped according to leaf color. Unless otherwise stated, those named enjoy shade to partial sun.

Blue shades The blue-leafed hostas need fairly heavy shade to maintain coloration in hot climates. *Hosta* 'Krossa Regal' has frosty blue leaves that grow 8 inches long and 5 inches wide. It grows in a distinctly upright, vase-shaped form. It can reach 30 inches tall and wide. *Hosta sieboldiana* 'Elegans' has heavily textured, blue-gray rounded leaves that grow 13 inches long and 10 inches wide. Leaves become heavily corrugated as they mature. It reaches 30 inches tall and 48 inches wide.

Green shades *Hosta lancifolia* has small, spear-shaped, dark green leaves about 6 inches long, forming clumps about 1 foot high and 18 inches wide. *Hosta* 'Royal Standard' has glossy green leaves that are 8 inches long and 6 inches wide. It grows in a large, vase-shaped clump. It tolerates some drought and more sun than most hostas and grows to be 18 inches tall and 36 inches wide.

Yellow to gold shades *Hosta* 'August Moon' has heavily corrugated gold leaves that are 6 inches long and 5 inches wide. It reaches 20 inches tall and 30 inches wide. *Hosta* 'Sum and Substance' has glossy, golden, heavily textured leaves that grow 20 inches long and 15 inches wide. It forms an impressive 30-inch-tall, 60-inch-wide mound.

Cream to gold margins *Hosta fortunei* 'Aureo-marginata' has glossy dark green leaves with irregular, yellow margins that grow 8 inches long and 5 inches wide. It reaches 16 inches tall and 24 inches wide. *Hosta* 'Frances Williams' has puckered blue-green leaves with broad, golden-yellow margins that deepen in color as the summer progresses. Leaves are 8 inches wide and 10 inches long. Plants grow 24 inches tall and 36 inches wide. *Hosta* 'Golden Tiara' has textured green leaves with gold borders that are 4 inches long and 2 to 3 inches wide. Plants grow 14 inches tall and 20 inches wide.

White margins *Hosta* 'Allan P. McConnell' has narrow, 3-inch-long, 2-inch-wide green leaves with a white margin. It forms an 8-inch tall, 18-inch-wide compact clump and is good for edging. *Hosta fortunei* 'Francee' has dark green leaves with crisp, white margins. Leaves are 7 inches long and 5 inches wide. Clumps grow 24 inches tall and 36 inches wide. *Hosta* 'Patriot' is a sought-after variety with hunter green centers and wide, irregular white margins. It grows 24 inches tall and 36 inches wide.

Hyssop, Anise Hyssop
Agastache species

The genus *Agastache* includes 20 or more species of varying appearance and cold hardiness. Many are native to the American Southwest and Mexico. Most are fragrant and smell like licorice. All are excellent nectar sources for butterflies and hummingbirds.

ZONE: Varies by type.

DESCRIPTION: These herblike perennials are showy and somewhat tender. Most are bushy and sport long, airy spikes of brightly colored, tubular-shaped flowers that bloom in late summer or early fall. Most types are hardy through USDA Zone 6.

EASY-CARE GROWING: Hyssop grows easily in well-drained, alkaline soil and is adapted to rocky soil. Some types are very drought tolerant but all flower better if they receive adequate rainfall or supplemental water. Hyssop will not tolerate wet soil in the winter. They love hot weather and grow best in areas with warm summers.

PROPAGATION: By seed.

USES: Mix with other sun-loving perennials such as Russian sage, butterfly bush, yarrow, blue mist spirea, and boltonia. This is an excellent plant for attracting hummingbirds and butterflies.

RELATED SPECIES AND VARIETIES: *Agastache cana*, Texas hummingbird mint, has raspberry pink flowers. It grows 24 to 36 inches tall and 18 inches wide, through Zone 5. *Agastache* x 'Blue Fortune' bears large, 5-inch-long powder blue flower spikes for many weeks through Zone 6. *Agastache rupestris*, licorice mint or sunset hyssop, blooms midsummer through fall up through Zone 5 with spikes of two-toned orange and purple flowers. 'Tutti Frutti' has a wonderful fruity-sweet scent.

RIS
Iris species

Although most gardeners are familiar with the bearded iris—also known as German iris—this large genus contains over 200 different species. The plants sport a marvelous array of flowers plus, in many cases, fine foliage. The genus name is derived from the ancient Greek word for "rainbow," referring to the many colors of the flowers.

ZONE: USDA 4.

DESCRIPTION: Irises usually have basal leaves in two ranks, linear to sword-shaped, often resembling a fan, arising from a thick rootstock (or rhizome) or, in some species, from a bulb. There are three groups in the rhizomatous species: Bearded iris has a "beard" or pattern of hairs on the bottom half of the falls (the lower petals); the crested iris has a cockscomblike crest on the falls; and the beardless iris doesn't have hairs on the bottom petals. They come in shades of pink, blue, lilac, purple to brown, yellow, orange, dark to almost black, and white. The only color that is absent is red.

EASY-CARE GROWING: Most irises need sunlight. All—except for a few noted exceptions—prefer well-drained soil. Water flag (*Iris pseudacorus*) delights in a watery spot and the Japanese iris (*I. ensata*) wants a humus-rich, moist soil. In the North, rhizomatous irises should have the tops of the rhizome showing when planted; in the South, they should be planted slightly deeper. The fan of leaves should be pointed in the direction you wish the plants to grow.

PROPAGATION: By division or separating the rhizomes.

USES: Even though bloom period is short, a bed of irises is ideal for a flower garden. There are irises for beside the pool, in the wild or woodland garden, in the early spring bulb bed, and for the rock garden. They make excellent cut flowers.

RELATED SPECIES: Tall, bearded iris, hardy to USDA 4, comes in a multitude of color combinations and sizes, with hundreds of new varieties introduced every year. The fanlike leaves are a lovely gray-green, browning at the tips in the heat of summer. There are varieties that bloom both in the spring and the fall. Tall, bearded irises are over 25 inches tall; intermediate bearded ones are between 16 and 27 inches; the standard plants are between 8 and 16 inches; and the miniatures grow to 8 inches tall. As with daylilies and hostas, there is a bewildering number of varieties and colors. Perhaps the best suggestion for the beginning gardener is to order a mix of colors, a choice frequently offered by most nurseries. *Iris cristata*, the dwarf crested iris that is hardy in USDA 5, wants partial shade and a humus-rich soil. It blooms in early spring in lavender-blue with a 2-inch, yellow crest across a 6-inch stem. Plants grow well in the woodland garden where they get partial shade. *Iris ensata* is the Japanese iris. They are hardy in USDA 4. Blossoms are often over 6 inches and resemble layers of colored linen waving in the wind. They bloom in June and prefer evenly moist, humus-rich soil. *Iris pseudacorus*, the yellow flag, blooms in late May to June with large yellow flowers on 40-inch stems. It is a beautiful plant for the bog or at the edge of a pond or pool. Yellow flag will also grow in drier soil as long as irrigation is provided. *Iris sibirica*, the Siberian iris, is native to moist meadows. Elegant 3- to 4-inch flowers are usually deep blue or purple on 30-inch stems. Unlike some of the other iris species, their foliage looks great all season—swordlike leaves stand erect and eventually form a large clump. They need full sun, prefer a good, moist soil, and are hardy in USDA 3. *Iris tectorum*, the Japanese roof iris, is reportedly used as a living binding material for thatched roofs in China and Japan. Plants are hardy in USDA 5, grow about 1 foot high, and are covered in June with 6-inch, lilac-blue flowers. They like full sun and moist soil.

JOE PYE WEED, SPOTTED JOE PYE WEED

Eupatorium maculatum, E. purpureum

Joe Pye weed is a North American wildflower that is enjoying a resurgence in popularity for use in the perennial garden. They are butterfly magnets when they bloom in late summer.

ZONE: USDA 4.

DESCRIPTION: Leaves are large (8 to 12 inches long), coarsely toothed, and arranged in whorls along the stem. They smell like vanilla when crushed. The large flower heads are 12 to 18 inches across and are packed with hundreds of small, purplish-pink flowers. *Eupatorium purpureum* has green stems, grows 4 to 7 feet tall and 3 feet wide, and is hardy to USDA Zone 4. Spotted Joe Pye weed, *E. maculatum*, looks very similar to *E. purpureum* except the stems are splashed with purple mottling. It is also cold-hardy to Zone 3. Both flower in late summer or early fall.

EASY-CARE GROWING: Moist, well-drained soil in full sun or partial shade is best for Joe Pye weed. Partial shade is especially important in regions with hot summers or in gardens with soil that is on the dry side. It takes two or three years for plants to get established. Once established, they are long-lived.

PROPAGATION: By division.

USES: Joe Pye weed is a stunning plant when used as a hedge at the back of a large garden or when used as a single specimen plant. Butterflies flock to the flowers.

RELATED VARIETIES: *Eupatorium purpureum* 'Big Umbrella' grows 7 feet tall and 2 to 3 feet wide. 'Atropurpureum' is a stately cultivar of *E. maculatum* with purple leaves, flowers, and stems on the upper portion of the plant. 'Gateway' is a shorter cultivar, growing 5 feet tall.

RELATED SPECIES: The hardy ageratum, *E. coelestinum,* grows 2 to 3 feet tall and bears dense blue flower heads in fall. Grow in moist soil and full sun.

JUPITER'S BEARD, RED VALERIAN
Centranthus ruber

Described as a "cheerful and blowzy plant," this old-fashioned garden plant first turned up in England in the sixteenth century. Plants are often sold as *V. coccineus*.

ZONE: USDA 5.

DESCRIPTION: Fragrant, ½-inch scarlet to red flowers grow in dense clusters on 2- to 3-foot stems. They begin blooming in spring and continue over a long period if old flowering stems are removed.

EASY-CARE GROWING: Red valerian is not fussy, needing only well-drained soil in full sun, although they will tolerate slight shade. Alkaline soil promotes the best growth. Plants do not grow well if the soil is overly rich. Flowering stems should be cut down to promote new flowers. If flowering stops due to hot summer weather, shear plants back by one-half to one-third to promote another round of bloom in late summer. Valerian self-sows readily and seedlings pop up all over the garden. If this is not desirable, simply hoe or pull out unwanted plants or remove old flowers before they can form seeds.

PROPAGATION: By division or seed.

USES: This plant is best when massed and is often naturalized along old walls and rock outcrops. It makes a long-lasting cut flower and is a good plant to supply butterflies with nectar.

RELATED VARIETIES: *Centranthus ruber* var. *alba* has white flowers; *C. ruber* var. *coccineus* has deep red flowers; and *C. ruber* var. *roseus* bears rose-colored flowers.

LADYBELLS
Adenophora species

Ladybells are often confused with campanulas, although they differ in subtle botanical characteristics. Ladybells tolerate heat better than campanulas and can be used as a replacement in southern gardens.

ZONE: USDA 3.

DESCRIPTION: Tall, 24- to 30-inch spires of dark blue, bell-shaped flowers bloom in mid- to late summer. These flowers are often found in old gardens, as they persist for years.

EASY-CARE GROWING: Ladybells are easy to grow, but their fleshy roots defy division. Plants need full sun or partial shade. They self-seed and spread quickly enough to be considered weedy. Keep ladybells in check by digging out sections of plants that are becoming invasive in early spring.

PROPAGATION: By seed.

USES: Ladybells have such beautiful blue flowers that they are welcome additions to the summer garden. They are also an excellent choice for the lightly shaded woodland garden.

RELATED SPECIES: *Adenophora confusa*, common ladybells, have deep blue nodding flowers in late spring for about four weeks. They grow 24 to 30 inches high. *Adenophora liliifolia*, lilyleaf ladybells, grow 18 to 24 inches tall and have pale blue or creamy flowers.

LADY'S MANTLE
Alchemilla mollis

Lady's mantles are beautiful plants usually grown for both their foliage and their unusual chartreuse flowers. They make a great ground cover and mix well with other plants in a lightly shaded garden.

ZONE: USDA 4.

DESCRIPTION: Plants grow about 14 inches high, with lobed leaves of gray-green that bear silky hairs. The leaves are almost waxy; small droplets of water bead up on the leaf after a rain. Clusters of chartreuse flowers are held on wiry stems above the leaves.

EASY-CARE GROWING: Lady's mantles are easy to grow if they receive partial shade and moist soil. They prefer regions with cool, moist summers but grow well in warmer climates if given consistent moisture and protection from hot sun. As the summer progresses, the plants become larger and have a tendency to flop. Flowers should be removed before the seeds ripen. Lady's mantle reseeds easily.

PROPAGATION: By seed or division in spring.

USES: The flowers appear in clusters in early summer, standing well above the leaves, and last for several weeks. They are excellent when cut and used in arrangements. These plants can be used in the front of the garden border or along the edge of a low wall where the leaves are easy to see. They can also be naturalized in large drifts.

RELATED SPECIES: *Alchemilla alpina*, the alpine lady's mantle, grows about 8 inches high and *Alchemilla erythropoda* grows about 6 inches high and has red stems.

LAMB'S-EARS
Stachys byzantina

Some plants beg to have a finger run along their surface. Among such plants, lamb's-ears is one of the best. The common name is precisely on the mark, since the gray-white, woolly leaves feel exactly like a lamb's skin.

ZONE: USDA 5.

DESCRIPTION: The 4-inch-long leaves and sturdy stems of this plant are covered with dense, white wool. Plants grow to about 6 inches tall. Flower spikes up to 2 feet tall bear small, pink to purple flowers hidden by silvery bracts. Flowers are not especially attractive and are often removed before they completely develop.

EASY-CARE GROWING: Lamb's-ears require good drainage and moist soil. As with many silver, fuzzy-leaved plants, they will rot if the crown stays wet or if grown in areas of the south with prolonged high humidity. Full sun or partial shade is fine. If the foliage starts to look bad in late summer, cut it back to the base and fresh leaves will emerge and look good until the end of the season.

PROPAGATION: By division in spring.

USES: Try this plant along the edge of a sunny border, in the rock garden, or as an effective ground cover. Even though the flowers are insignificant, the dried spikes are very effective in dried arrangements. Lamb's-ears also does well in pots for terrace decoration.

RELATED VARIETY: 'Helen von Stein' (known as 'Big Ears') has very large leaves and tolerates heat well. 'Silver Carpet' is a non-flowering form of the same plant.

LAVENDER
Lavandula angustifolia

Lavender is an aromatic herb native to Mediterranean areas. Ancient Greeks and Romans used pieces of the sweetly scented plant in bathing water and as a perfume. Its fragrance is still valued—lavender is a popular ingredient in soap, perfume, and sachets.

ZONE: USDA 6.

DESCRIPTION: Plants are shrubby, with multiple stems that are square and narrow. Evergreen leaves are white and woolly when young. Flower spikes end in terminal clusters of lavender or dark purple flowers, blooming in late June and bearing a pleasing scent. In warm climates, lavender can grow 2 to 3 feet tall and 3 feet wide.

EASY-CARE GROWING: Lavender thrives in full sun and well-drained, slightly alkaline, sandy soil. It is very drought tolerant. Plants do not grow well in areas with high humidity. They rot in poorly drained soil and are especially susceptible to rot in wet winter soil. Do not prune plants in fall or winter—wait until new growth is showing in the spring, then cut back dead wood.

PROPAGATION: Take 3- to 4-inch stem cuttings from nonflowering stems and be sure to include a "heel" of older wood too. (A cutting with a heel is a stem of the current year's growth with a small piece of the previous year's growth at the base.) Lavender can also be propagated by seed but germination can be erratic.

USES: Lavender is a mainstay in herb gardens and in gardens designed to emphasize fragrance. It is frequently used as a low hedge because it can be sheared and shaped for formal designs. Lavender also looks good when used as an individual clump in rock gardens. It is also suitable in front of stone walls that face away from the wind. Flower stems can be cut for fresh or dried arrangements.

RELATED VARIETIES: 'Hidcote' has deep violet flowers on 20-inch shrubs and 'Munstead Dwarf,' a shorter type, has deep purple flowers at a 12-inch height. 'Provence' has lavender-blue flowers and is reported to be the most cold-hardy variety.

LEADWORT, PLUMBAGO
Ceratostigma plumbaginoides

Leadwort is a highly underrated ground cover of great beauty and considerable late-season interest. It is durable and long-lived and requires very little maintenance. The only drawbacks are that it is not evergreen—except in the southern regions (Zones 8 and 9)—and that it is slow to emerge in the spring. However, once leadwort breaks dormancy it grows rapidly.

ZONE: USDA 5.

DESCRIPTION: This perennial is a deciduous or semi-evergreen ground cover that grows 6 to 10 inches tall. It has glossy green leaves on long, trailing stems and bears gentian-blue flowers. The ¾-inch diameter flowers begin in early August and continue until frost. The foliage turns a lovely reddish bronze after the first frost and persists well into winter.

EASY-CARE GROWING: Plant in well-drained soil that is rich in organic matter. Leadwort likes full sun or part shade. It will rot if the soil stays too wet, especially in winter. In most of Zones 5 and 6 plants die to the ground in winter. Apply a light winter mulch, and wait until growth resumes in mid-spring to cut stems back to the ground. Plant only in the spring: Leadwort needs a full growing season to get roots established.

PROPAGATION: By division in the spring.

USES: Plant as a ground cover under shrubs and small trees and interplant spring-blooming bulbs such as crocus and daffodils. Leadwort should not be combined with other perennials because it tends to outgrow neighboring plants.

LENTEN ROSE, HELLEBORE
Helleborus orientalis

*L*enten rose is one of the earliest, if not *the* earliest, perennial to flower in the garden. These evergreen beauties are easy to grow and no self-respecting shade garden should be without several clumps.

ZONE: USDA 4.

DESCRIPTION: Deeply divided, palmate evergreen leaves grow from a thick rootstock, producing nodding flowers that appear in late winter or early spring. Flowers easily last for 8 to 10 weeks and are either whitish or plum-colored. Plants grow 15 inches tall and wide.

EASY-CARE GROWING: Lenten rose grows easily in deep, well-drained soil with plenty of humus and partial shade. It likes consistent moisture and alkaline soil. Plants are slow to establish but are long-lived after the second year. At low temperatures, some protection is needed against drying wind. A light mulch of ground oak leaves helps keep the evergreen leaves looking good through winter. If leaves are damaged, prune them off in late winter to make way for fresh growth.

PROPAGATION: By digging and replanting small seedlings that appear at the base of two- to three-year-old plants.

USES: The foliage alone is worth growing and makes an excellent ground cover. Lenten rose can also be effectively mixed in with hosta, ferns, brunnera, and heuchera in shaded gardens. Flowers are good for cutting.

RELATED SPECIES: *Helleborus foetidus*, bearsfoot hellebore, is hardy to Zone 5 and has deeply divided, narrow, dark green leaflets. Light green nodding flowers bloom in early spring. Plants grow 18 to 24 inches tall and 18 inches wide.

LILY

Lilium species

With over 80 species and hundreds of varieties, the lily family varies greatly in appearance. The North American Lily Society arranges various types of lilies into nine separate horticultural divisions according to flower and plant shape, parentage, and time of bloom. Of the nine divisions, there are three that fit our "easy care" requirements—Asiatics, Aurelian hybrids, and Martagons. While Oriental lilies are frequently planted in the garden, they don't like the hot summer temperatures in most of the United States. Oriental lilies are best left to the commercial growers who supply cut flowers to florists.

ZONES: USDA 3 to 5.

DESCRIPTION: Asiatic hybrid lilies usually have upward-facing flowers and grow 1 to 3 feet tall. They flower early in the season. The color range is broad but the most common colors are red, orange, and yellow. Flowers are generally unscented. Aurelian hybrids have fragrant, trumpet-shaped flowers and bloom in July and August. They can grow 6 feet tall and require sturdy stakes. Martagon hybrids grow 3 to 4 feet tall and bear many small (1- to 2-inch) turkscap blooms. Flowers are usually purplish-red or white. These lilies prefer partial shade although they will tolerate full sun or deep shade.

EASY-CARE GROWING: Good drainage is absolutely essential—bulbs rot easily in soil that stays wet for too long. Plant most types in full sun or part shade in soil that is rich in organic matter. Mulch organic matter around emerging shoots in the spring. Stake tall-growing types so they don't topple over in heavy rain or wind.

PROPAGATION: By division or removing stem bulbils (small bulbs that develop along the stem). Pot bulbils and grow for one year before planting in the garden.

USES: Plant in groups of three or more for maximum effect. Use as cut flowers in fresh arrangements.

RELATED VARIETIES: A few of the good Asiatic varieties include 'Enchantment' (orange), 'Connecticut King' (yellow), and 'Iowa Rose' (pink).

LILY TURF
Liriope muscari

Lily turf is a grasslike plant belonging to the lily family. It is often used as a low-maintenance ground cover because it is oblivious to heat, drought, high humidity, and pests. Lily turf is usually evergreen.

ZONE: USDA 6.

DESCRIPTION: Dark green, strappish leaves are 1 to 1½ inches wide and grow in 12- to 18-inch-tall arched mounds. Violet or dark blue flower spikes are produced in late summer and are followed by black seed heads.

EASY-CARE GROWING: Liriope grows well in any good, well-drained soil—in either sun or shade. Plantings should be sheared or mowed to the ground in late winter to encourage vigorous growth.

PROPAGATION: By division in early spring.

USES: Liriope is unmatched as an easy-care ground cover. It is also excellent when used to edge a path or walkway.

RELATED VARIETIES: 'Big Blue' has very wide leaves and lavender flowers. 'Christmas Tree' has

lilac flowers that are very wide at the base and much narrower at the top. 'Munroe's White' has white flowers, prefers shade, and is slower growing than purple-flowered varieties. 'Variegata' has creamy margins and spreads more slowly than nonvariegated types.

RELATED SPECIES: *Liriope spicata*, creeping liriope, is cold-hardy to Zone 4. It grows 12 to 18 inches tall and has narrower leaves (¼ inch wide) than *L. muscari*. Foliage turns yellow in the winter.

LUPINE
Lupinus hybrids

Fields of native lupines growing in Texas, Colorado, and California are a beautiful sight. Over 70 species of lupine grow throughout the United States. Unfortunately, many of the native varieties are hard to propagate and don't take kindly to being grown in containers. Lupines tend to be a bit finicky about where they grow but, for those willing to try, the Russell hybrids are readily available.

ZONE: USDA 4.

DESCRIPTION: Attractive alternate, cool green leaves are fingerlike, with many leaflets beginning at a central point. In early summer, plants produce 30-inch spikes of picture-perfect flowers followed by silky seedpods. Flowers may be pink, purple, white, cream, red, blue, or bicolored.

EASY-CARE GROWING: Lupines require a lot of water and a spot in full sun or in the lightest of shade. Plants resent areas with hot summers. Soil must be well drained with additional grit or sand. Lupines like acidic soil. Plant one-gallon-size plants in the fall in Zones 5 and farther south. Mulch in summer to keep roots cool; provide winter mulch if snow cover is not reliable. At best, they are short-lived perennials and in areas with hot summers they should be treated as a fall-planted, spring-blooming annual. In areas with cooler summers, they will live for two or three years. Deadhead to prevent seed formation and to conserve the plant's strength. Cutting back to the ground after flowering will often produce a second crop of blossoms.

PROPAGATION: By seed.

USES: Lupines should be planted in large groups where the flowers make a spectacular show. The plants are especially suited to seaside gardens.

RELATED VARIETIES: The Russell strain of lupines is the variety usually offered by nurseries. They can be purchased in several color combinations including blue, pink, red, purple, maroon, white, and mixed.

CAROLINA LUPINE, SOUTHERN LUPINE
Thermopsis villosa (syn. *Thermopsis caroliniana*)

Carolina lupines are native American wildflowers originally from North Carolina and Georgia. They closely resemble *Baptisia australis*—false indigo—and both are members of the pea family. The genus is Greek for "resembling a lupine," which they do. False lupine is a beautiful garden plant that offers a nice contrast to spring blooming bulbs.

ZONE: USDA 3.

DESCRIPTION: Leaves are blue-green with three leaflets on stems growing to 3 or 4 feet tall. Yellow, pealike flowers bloom in April or May on 6- to 12-inch-long spikes and persist for three or four weeks. Flowers are followed by pods resembling small string beans covered with short hairs.

EASY-CARE GROWING: Plants grow in almost any good, well-drained soil in full sun or light shade in the South. Flower stems may need to be staked if grown in light shade. In rich soil, plants will be very tall and need staking. New plants take a few years to form sizable clumps but are very long-lived once established. Plants are very drought-resistant if they are given adequate moisture just before flowering begins. Cut plants back to the ground if the foliage declines in midsummer.

PROPAGATION: By seed (it must be fresh).

USES: The spires of yellow flowers are very attractive against a dark background, so keep them at the back of the border—especially in front of bushes or shrubbery.

RELATED SPECIES: *Thermopsis lupinoides* (syn *T. lanceolata*), false lupine, grows 9 to 12 inches tall and produces spikes of lemon yellow flowers in late spring. This species is native to northern regions and dislikes summer heat. *Thermopsis montana*, mountain thermopsis, grows to 2 feet and grows naturally in western states.

MEADOW RUE

Thalictrum aquilegiifolium

Meadow rue is a tall and lovely plant with flowers that lack petals but have dozens of fluffy stamens. The English word "rue" refers to the resemblance between the leaves of these plants and the herb rue (*Ruta*).

ZONE: USDA 5.

DESCRIPTION: The blue-green leaves are compound and look like columbine leaves. Leaves extend from stout-branched stalks growing up to 3 feet tall. Plants bear clusters of rosy purple flowers with many stamens, resembling delicate balls of fluff. They bloom in late May and June.

EASY-CARE GROWING: Soil for meadow rue should be moist with plenty of additional organic matter in partial shade. In cool northern gardens they can take full sun. In areas that have hot summers they must have additional moisture. Meadow rue is heat tolerant. If foliage gets ragged after flowering, cut plants back to the ground and keep well watered until new growth appears.

PROPAGATION: By division in early spring or seed.

USES: Use these plants in the wild garden where they naturalize with ease. They are also excellent as filler plants at the back of a bed or border. Both flowers and foliage are good for bouquets.

RELATED VARIETY: 'White Cloud' has white flowers.

RELATED SPECIES: *Thalictrum delavayi* 'Hewitt's Double' blooms in summer with double lilac flowers that are very full. *Thalictrum rochebrunianum* 'Lavender Mist' has violet flowers with gold stamens. It grows 5 to 6 feet tall and should be planted in groups of three. *T. rochebrunianum* may be short-lived. *Thalictrum kiusianum* only grows 4 inches tall and is delightful as an edging plant in front of small hostas. It has airy clusters of pinkish flowers all summer.

MEADOWSWEET, QUEEN-OF-THE-PRAIRIE
Filipendula rubra

Meadowsweet is an American native at home at the edge of woods, in wet prairies, and in meadows from New York to Minnesota and south.

ZONE: USDA 3.

DESCRIPTION: Meadowsweet is a big plant, growing to 7 feet tall and 4 feet wide, with large clusters of tiny, pinkish-peach flowers. A plant in bloom resembles a ball of cotton candy. Flowers sit on top of stout stems and bloom in July.

EASY-CARE GROWING: Meadowsweet prefers an alkaline, well-drained, moist garden soil in full sun—although they will succeed in partial shade. Plants eventually will form a good-sized clump. Leave old flowers on the plants since deadheading does not promote rebloom, and the dried flower heads are ornamental. If foliage becomes ragged in late summer, cut plants to the ground and keep the soil consistently moist until new growth occurs.

PROPAGATION: By seed or division in early spring or fall.

USES: Meadowsweet is best toward the back of a border or against a dark background such as low trees or shrubs. It can be used effectively as a single specimen plant.

RELATED SPECIES: *Filipendula purpurea*, Japanese meadowsweet, bears deep-pink flower clusters and crimson stems. *Filipendula ulmaria* grows between 3 and 6 feet tall. Creamy white flowers resemble feathery plumes and appear in June. 'Flore Pleno' has showy, double flowers. *Filipendula vulgaris* (syn. *F. hexapetala*) has finely cut, fernlike leaves and bears loose panicles of small, white flowers on 18-inch stems. The roots are tuberous and spread almost like a ground cover.

MONKSHOOD
Aconitum napellus

Monkshood has been in cultivation for a very long time. Herbalists were writing about its toxic properties as early as the sixteenth century. It is a lovely addition to the back of the perennial border but all parts of the plant are extremely poisonous. Be sure to wash your hands after pruning plants.

ZONE: USDA 3.

DESCRIPTION: Showy dark blue flower spikes open in late summer or early fall. Individual flowers are shaped like a helmet or a hood. The leaves resemble delphinium foliage. Plants grow 3 to 4 feet tall.

EASY-CARE GROWING: Aconitum grows best where night temperatures regularly fall below 70°F. Plant in full sun in cooler regions. Provide afternoon shade in warmer regions. Soil should be high in organic matter and moist but not swampy. Plant tubers early enough in the fall so that the roots have time to get established before the frost. Set the crowns just below the surface and do not disturb plants after they have been placed in the garden. Monkshood is long-lived and does not react well to division or transplanting.

PROPAGATION: By seed (it must be fresh).

USES: Use in groups of three or five at the back of the garden. Monkshood makes an excellent cut flower but be careful not to get its sap on cuts or wounds.

RELATED VARIETIES: 'Bressingham Spire' has compact stems with deep violet-blue flowers on 3-foot-tall stems that bloom from midsummer through fall. 'Carneum' has pale rose-pink flowers on 4- to 5-foot stems. Flower color is best in cool climates.

OBEDIENT PLANT, FALSE DRAGONHEAD
Physostegia virginiana

A member of the mint family, obedient plants are native to the eastern United States. Florets are arranged on the four-sided stems in rigidly vertical lines. These florets can be gently turned with your finger so they face a particular direction, perhaps giving rise to the name "obedient."

ZONE: USDA 3.

DESCRIPTION: Basal rosettes of foliage are evergreen in milder climates. Square, strong stems are from 1 to 3 feet tall and have narrow, toothed leaves, bearing 12-inch spikes of rose-purple flowers that resemble a snapdragon. Plants flower in August and September. Obedient plants grow from 2 to 4 feet tall and spread to 3 feet wide.

EASY-CARE GROWING: Physostegia likes full sun and will tolerate most soils, preferring the addition of moisture-retentive organic matter. It is at its best in moist conditions. Plants may need to be staked, especially if grown in shade. Physostegia is invasive (in rich soil it can be very invasive) and should be either fenced at ground level or divided every two years to keep it in control.

PROPAGATION: By division in spring or seed.

USES: Because they flower late in the season, these are valuable plants for beds and borders. They will often bloom into October. They should be planted in groups and are excellent for naturalizing in the wild garden where rampant growth does not pose a problem. Physostegia makes an excellent cut flower.

RELATED VARIETIES: 'Alba' is pure white. 'Pink Bouquet' is a beautiful 3- to 4-foot, bright pink selection that requires staking. 'Summer Snow' is a clean white selection that is a little less invasive than the species. 'Vivid' is 24 to 36 inches high with flowers of a brilliant lavender-pink. Plants are compact and upright.

ORNAMENTAL ONION
Allium species

There are over 500 known species of allium. This group covers plants that are strictly ornamental as well as edible onions, garlic, and chives

ZONE: Varies according to species.

DESCRIPTION: The ornamental types range in size from 3 inches to 4 feet tall. The flowers are rounded and vary in color, including purple, pink, white, mauve, and greenish. Most have straplike leaves and seed heads that remain attractive after plants finish blooming. Many of the ornamental onions have a pungent odor when crushed.

EASY-CARE GROWING: Plant in full sun in well-drained, alkaline soil that is rich in organic matter. Provide ½ inch of water per week during the growing season. Allium is drought-tolerant at other times. Most alliums self-seed and some species such as garlic chives (*A. tuberosum*) and drumstick allium (*A. sphaerocephalum*) can become invasive. If this is not desirable, remove old flower heads before they go to seed. Some species of allium go dormant after flowering. It is normal for their leaves to turn yellow and die back to the ground during or immediately after flowering. They will reemerge the following spring. If you are growing types that go dormant after flowering, place taller allium varieties at the back of the garden behind or between other plants. As the foliage dies down, the surrounding plants will hide the bare spots. Remove the leaves after they turn brown.

PROPAGATION: By division of bulbs that form from the mother bulbs.

USES: Plant in groups of three or more in combination with other perennials.

RELATED SPECIES AND VARIETIES: *Allium* 'Globemaster' is a vigorous plant with stout 2½-foot stems supporting deep lavender flowers that get 4 to 6 inches across. Plants bloom for many weeks with newer blossoms replacing those that fade. It is an excellent cut flower and the seed heads are ornamental. *Allium sphaerocephalum*, drumstick chives, grow 18 to 36 inches tall and bear 2-inch purple flower heads that open in June and last for three weeks. This variety grows very well in hot climates (through Zone 8). Cut flowers last for around ten days.

ORANGE CONEFLOWER, CONEFLOWER, BLACK-EYED SUSAN
Rudbeckia species

All the members of the genus are native American wildflowers, known collectively as coneflowers. Rudbeckia is comprised of about 30 species including annuals, biennials, and perennials.

ZONE: USDA 5.

DESCRIPTION: Coneflowers have hairy, 2- to 3-foot stems with simple, saw-toothed edges. They bear daisies with yellow ray flowers and purple-brown disk flowers. Depending on the species, they begin blooming in June and on through the growing season.

EASY-CARE GROWING: Although best with a good, moist soil, orange coneflowers will adapt to any good garden soil that is not too dry or too wet. It prefers full sun. Divide plants every three years.

PROPAGATION: By division or seed.

USES: Great flowers for the wild garden or for naturalizing in the meadow garden, 'Goldsturm' is best for the formal bed or border and should be planted in drifts. These flowers are perfect when used in combination with ornamental grasses. They are excellent for cutting and are good nectar sources for butterflies. Birds feast on the seed heads.

RELATED SPECIES AND VARIETIES: *Rudbeckia fulgida* is known as orange coneflower. The most common cultivar is 'Goldsturm.' It grows about 24 inches high and is most happy in full sun and moist soil. The golden-yellow flowers bloom profusely in July and August. Plants form large clumps and spread by seed and underground rhizomes. *Rudbeckia laciniata*, the cutleaf or green-headed coneflower, is valuable for a wild garden and begins blooming in June. It likes moist soil and full sun. 'Goldquelle' or, as it's sometimes called 'Gold Drop,' has big, double flowers on 24- to 30-inch stems. 'Herbstonne' grows up to 7 feet tall and is stunning at the back of the garden. *Rudbeckia triloba*, commonly called three-lobed coneflower or brown-eyed Susan, begins blooming in June. It bears hundreds of 1½-inch yellow flowers and is quite showy. It tends to be a biennial but self-seeds reliably.

PACHYSANDRA, JAPANESE SPURGE

Pachysandra terminalis

Pachysandra is the quintessential ground cover. It grows easily under trees where many other plants can't compete for light, food, and water.

ZONE: USDA 4.

DESCRIPTION: Fleshy stems, 6 to 9 inches tall, have simple, toothed, evergreen leaves. These are often crowded at the tips of branches, which bear small, greenish-white flowers in erect spikes in the spring. Plants spread by rhizomes and can quickly cover a large area.

EASY-CARE GROWING: Any good, moist garden soil is sufficient for pachysandra. The plants are especially valuable since they will grow in shady areas where few other plants survive. The leaves will yellow in full sun.

PROPAGATION: By division or stem cuttings.

USES: Pachysandra is great under shrubs and in open shade under trees. It can be used to carpet banks and as an edging along shaded walkways. Plants can also be set in pots for the terrace.

RELATED VARIETY: 'Green Carpet' grows 6 inches tall and has darker green leaves than the species. 'Silveredge' has a narrow, silvery white edge around leaf margins.

RELATED SPECIES: *Pachysandra procumbens*, or Allegheny spurge, is a native American plant that is usually evergreen as far north as Zone 5. Stems have a purplish tinge and bear toothed leaves flecked with silver that becomes more pronounced in the spring. The spring flowers are off-white and quite beautiful. Allegheny spurge does not spread as vigorously as Japanese spurge and can be used where smaller clumps are desired.

PEONY
Paeonia species

Peonies have been loved throughout history—they have inspired poetry and been the subjects of tapestry and wall paintings. Not only are peony flowers beautiful, the plants themselves are especially attractive and they function as a small shrub with handsome foliage when they are not in flower. Peonies are truly an easy-to-grow perennial. They are extremely cold hardy, they require very little care after they are established, and they bloom reliably. There are many colors and flower forms available.

ZONE: USDA 3.

DESCRIPTION: Herbaceous peonies are shrubby plants with thick roots and large, compound, glossy green leaves on strong stems. They bear showy flowers with a pleasing fragrance. The blooms are followed by large, interesting seedpods. Flower forms include Japanese/anemone (single petals and obvious stamens); semi-double (double petals and showy center stamens that resemble petals); bomb double (many petals and rounded centers); and double (large petal-packed blooms). Ants, often seen in company with peony buds, feast on a sweet, sticky secretion that covers the buds. Ants do not hurt the plants. Herbaceous peonies die down to the ground for the winter. Tree peonies have branches with obvious bark. Like small trees, tree peonies remain in evidence all year and should not be cut down. Herbaceous peonies are classified in several ways. The most helpful classification divides peonies into three categories based on when they bloom.

Early-blooming types include those that open in early May (March or early April in the South). Pastels and patterns of multiple colors dominate this group.

Mid-season types bloom in mid-May and are usually brightly colored with clear hues of red or pink.

Late-season types open in late May and early June and include the widely recognized flower form of traditional heavy, double flowers.

EASY-CARE GROWING: Peony roots should be planted in the fall. Plant in full sun (light shade in the South) in a hole 18 inches wide and deep. Be sure the soil has ample organic matter and is well drained. If soil is excessively acid, add one cup of lime per plant. Keep manure and added fertilizers away from direct contact with the roots. Plant with the "eyes" (growing points) facing the top and about 1½ inches below the soil surface. Water well. Mulch the first year to protect from severe cold. Peonies grow and bloom much better on a regular fertilization schedule. Nutrients can be applied in the form of compost or well-rotted manure. A 2- or 3-inch layer of compost can be spread around peonies in the spring. A 2-inch layer of aged manure can be spread around plants in late fall. Do not use fresh manure, poultry manure, or rabbit manure—they are too rich in nitrogen. If a granular fertilizer is used, select one with a low nitrogen (N) ratio such as 5-10-10. Excessive nitrogen produces abundant foliage but few flowers. Fertilize in the fall or winter after the peony foliage has been removed. This will give the nutrients time to break down in the soil and become available to plants by the spring. Distribute the fertilizer in a ring around the drip line of the plant. Lightly fertilize plants the second fall after planting. By the third year, fertilize two times: in the late fall while plants are dormant and again at flowering time. Peonies must have a period of winter chilling to grow and flower properly. The dormancy requirement is met when soil temperature stays in a specific temperature range (usually around 40°F) over a specific period of time. Many peonies are hardy, thriving in the coldest areas of the United States. This considered, it might be surprising to know that many peonies also grow well as

far south as Zone 7. While not all varieties are equally at home in warmer climates, many grow and bloom. Gardeners in the South should consider early- to mid-season blooming cultivars such as 'Red Glory,' 'America,' and 'Red Charm.' Later-flowering varieties develop weak stems and are more susceptible to diseases as temperatures increase. Single-flowered or Japanese flower forms are also good bets.

PROPAGATION: By division of the roots in the fall or seed (seedlings will take three years or more to bloom).

USES: Peonies can be used as specimen plants, in hedges, beds or borders, and in the cutting garden—they are delightful in almost any capacity. Remember that even if they did not bloom in a particular year, the attractive shape and gloss of the leaves and their shrubby aspect make peonies valuable.

GARDEN PHLOX, TALL PHLOX
Phlox paniculata

Phlox are very popular plants since they are easy to grow, great for color, and marvelous for cutting. Selections should be made based on color preference and resistance to powdery mildew.

ZONE: USDA 5.

DESCRIPTION: Phlox form clumps that bear simple, lance-shaped leaves on very strong stems. These are topped with clusters of usually fragrant, showy, five-petaled flowers. They bloom over a long period.

EASY-CARE GROWING: Garden phlox need good, well-drained soil in full sun or light shade and plenty of water during the summer. Divide plants every three years to keep them vigorous and deadhead to prolong bloom. Plants are prone to an unsightly fungal disease called powdery mildew. White, feltlike dust covers the foliage, and sometimes the flowers. Plants rarely die but leaves may become distorted and drop. Powdery mildew is most prevalent when plants are grown in areas with poor air circulation. Outbreaks occur in mid- to late summer when warm days are followed by cool, humid nights. To reduce the problem, select mildew-resistant varieties and provide 18 inches between plants so air can circulate freely. Moderate but constant soil moisture during the growing season reduces powdery mildew. Also, a blast of water from the hose will help dislodge the spores. Do this early in the day so the foliage has plenty of time to dry before nightfall.

PROPAGATION: By division.

USES: Phlox can be bunched by color or mixed in the middle or back of a perennial garden. Phlox makes a very good cut flower.

RELATED VARIETIES: 'David' is a white variety that grows 40 inches tall. 'Bright Eyes' has pale pink flowers with a crimson eye. 'Franz Schubert' has lilac flowers and grows 30 inches tall. 'Starfire' is red and grows 30 inches tall. All have good mildew resistance.

RELATED SPECIES AND VARIETIES: *Phlox maculata*, known as wild sweet william or spotted phlox, looks much like *P. paniculata* but it is more mildew resistant. The primary differences between the two are that *P. maculata* blooms about two weeks earlier, has darker green leaves, and spotted stems. 'Miss Lingard' has white flowers; 'Omega' has white blooms with a lilac eye; and 'Rosalinde' has dark pink flowers.

MOSS PHLOX
Phlox subulata

When carpets of moss phlox bloom across America in April and May you know that spring is serious about staying. Another easy-to-grow perennial, moss phlox clings easily to steep banks, grows snugly against rocks, and cascades over rock walls with very little supervision from the gardener.

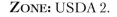

ZONE: USDA 2.

DESCRIPTION: Evergreen, dark green, prickly leaves grow on trailing stems. Groups of three to five 5-petaled, flat flowers are held above the foliage. Flowers may be blue, purple, pink, red, white, or striped. Plants grow 6 inches tall.

EASY-CARE GROWING: Moss phlox is not picky about soil but needs good drainage and full sun to flourish. After plants finish blooming, shear them back by one-half to encourage compact growth later in the season. As with all evergreen perennials, do not prune in the fall. Wait until spring to remove any foliage that has become damaged over the winter. Divide plants every three years after they bloom to keep them vigorous.

PROPAGATION: By division or layering. To layer, cover a piece of a nonflowering stem with 1 inch of soil and keep the soil moist. Roots will develop and the rooted stem can be removed and planted elsewhere.

USES: Plant in the rock garden, mix with spring-flowering bulbs, or use in clumps in the perennial garden. Moss phlox is not a good ground cover for large areas because it gets too thin.

RELATED VARIETIES: 'Candy Stripe' has colorful two-tone flowers of white and pink. 'Emerald Blue' has pale lilac blue flowers and good foliage. 'Millstream Daphne' has deep pink flowers with a dark eye. It is a vigorous grower, and compact. 'Pink Emerald' has long-blooming pink flowers.

PINCUSHION FLOWER
Scabiosa caucasica

The pincushion flower was introduced to England in 1591. It eventually made its way to America and has been a popular garden flower ever since. The common name refers to the flower heads—when they are closed they resemble pincushions full of pins.

ZONE: USDA 3.

DESCRIPTION: Plants have simple, lance-shaped, deeply cut leaves, with long, graceful flower stems growing to 2 feet high. They bear domed flower heads up to 3 inches across. Butterflies and bees find pincushion flower irresistible.

EASY-CARE GROWING: Plant in rich, well-drained garden soil in full sun. In areas of hot summers, light shade is welcomed. Plant in groups of three or more at the front of the garden to get the maximum effect from the delicate flowers. Remove dead flowers for a longer period of bloom.

PROPAGATION: By division in spring, or seed.

USES: Plant scabiosa in small drifts along the edge of the bed or border. They make excellent cut flowers that last for about seven days in fresh arrangements.

RELATED VARIETIES: 'Alba' has pure white flowers; 'Bressingham White' has 3-inch, clear white flowers on 3-inch stems; 'Fama' has lavender flowers with silver centers; 'House Hybrids' produce flowers about 2 inches in diameter in colors of blue, lavender, and white.

RELATED SPECIES: *Scabiosa columbaria* is more compact than *S. caucasica* and flowers for a longer period of time. 'Butterfly Blue' grows about 10 inches tall and bears light blue blooms. 'Pink Mist' produces lavender-pink flowers on 10-inch stems. They are excellent garden plants but do not tolerate poor drainage.

ORIENTAL POPPY
Papaver orientale

Groups of scarlet red poppies in American gardens are a cheerful sight in late spring. The Latin name, Papaver, is thought to refer to the sound the seeds made when chewing them.

ZONE: USDA 5.

DESCRIPTION: Basal leaves are covered with hairs. Graceful stalks grow to 4 feet and bear single or double flowers with petals of crepe paper texture surrounding many black stamens. Flowers are 4 inches across and marked in the center with a black eye. They flower in late May and June. Attractive seed pods form after the flowers fade. Any part of the plant will bleed a milky sap when cut.

EASY-CARE GROWING: Poppies are very easy to grow, wanting only good, well-drained soil in full sun. Drainage is especially important in the winter—excess water causes roots to rot. Plant dormant roots in the fall and place the crown 3 inches below the soil surface. Mulch the first winter to prevent heaving. Plants go dormant in late summer, so their spaces should be filled with annuals or summer bulbs. Alternatively, large, late-blooming perennials such as boltonia or perovskia can be planted nearby to cover the bare ground. New leaves usually reemerge in fall.

PROPAGATION: By division in the fall or by root cuttings in the spring.

USES: Use poppies in beds or borders in combination with other perennials or in single groupings where their summer dormancy does not cause an unsightly problem. Oriental poppies are good cut flowers if they are picked in bud and the cut ends are seared over a flame to prevent the milky sap from flowing out.

RELATED VARIETIES: 'Brilliant' has fiery red flowers; 'Carmen' bears deep red flowers; 'Harvest Moon' has double orange-yellow flowers; 'Queen Alexander' has salmon-pink flowers with black centers; 'Maiden's Blush' has ruffled petals of white with a blush-pink edge; and 'White King' is white.

Siebold Primrose, Japanese Star Primrose
Primula sieboldii

In the wild world of gardening there are over 400 species of primroses. Most primroses revel in an English climate that calls for cool temperatures and plenty of rainfall and are at a loss in the often short spring and variable summers found over much of the United States. However, *Primula sieboldii* has proven to be a good performer in the United States. The genus name is a diminutive of the Latin *primus*, "first," alluding to the early flowering of certain European species.

ZONE: USDA 5.

DESCRIPTION: The basal foliage is a rosette with dark green, heart-shaped leaves with a scalloped edge that grow 4 to 8 inches tall. The plant bears tight bunches of 1½-inch-wide, pink or purple flowers with white eyes on 12-inch stems that stand well above the foliage. Plants bloom in late spring.

EASY-CARE GROWING: Plant in partial shade and good, moist soil. Unlike other primroses, the leaves disappear and plants become dormant in the summer so the gardener is spared the rigor of worrying about drought and heat.

PROPAGATION: By seed or stem cuttings (after plants flower).

USES: Primroses are unexcelled for the woodland garden or for planting among spring wildflowers in a shady spot of the garden—even without bloom the foliage is very attractive. They make excellent cut flowers. Dormant plants may be potted up in late winter and forced into bloom at normal room temperatures.

RELATED VARIETIES: 'Geisha Girl' has clear light pink flowers; 'Mikado' is deep rose-pink; and 'Snowflake' has large, pure white flowers.

WALL ROCK CRESS, ROCK CRESS
Arabis caucasica

Arabis is a charming plant that is popular for use in rock gardens. It also looks great hanging down over the edge of rock walls.

ZONE: USDA 4.

DESCRIPTION: These creepers form large mats of gray-green leaves covered in a soft, white down. In spring, they send up flowering stems covered with dozens of four-petaled flowers, ½- to 1-inch-wide, with a sweet scent.

EASY-CARE GROWING: Plant in full sun in lean, well-drained, alkaline soil. Plants melt out in damp soil and in heat coupled with humidity. Plants should be sheared back by one-half after flowering to keep them from getting thin and ragged. Do not cut plants back in the fall; wait until new growth shows in the spring. Plants tend to be short-lived.

PROPAGATION: By division in early spring or fall, stem cuttings, or seed.

USES: Rock cress is best suited for a rock garden or for cultivation in a wall garden.

RELATED VARIETIES: 'Compinkie' has rosy pink flowers; 'Flore-plena' is the double, white-flowered form with 10-inch stems; and 'Snow Cap' is a large-flowered single form.

RELATED SPECIES: *Arabis ferdinandi-coburgi* 'Variegata,' Ferdinand's rock cress, bears white flowers on 5-inch stems and has green leaves mottled and edged in white. *Arabis procurens* has shiny, evergreen, rounded leaves. It grows better than *A. caucasica* in poor, dry soil and also takes to rich soil, in sun or light shade. The growth habit is more compact and the flowers are smaller and not as showy as *A. caucasica*.

ROCKCRESS
Aubretia deltoidea

Rockcresses are trailing perennials that burst into glorious bloom in late April and May. Plants originally came from Greece and Sicily.

ZONE: USDA 4.

DESCRIPTION: Aubretia is a creeping, trailing plant with small, simple leaves covered with tiny hairs. They bear a wealth of 4-petaled flowers, each about ¾-inch-wide and typically in blues, lilacs, and purples. Plant height is between 4 and 8 inches. The leaves are evergreen when given snow cover but turn brown without it. The growth habit is more compact than that of *Arabis caucasica*.

EASY-CARE GROWING: Rockcress prefers good soil with perfect drainage and a location in full sun. It also does well in light shade with a very lean soil mix that is quite sandy. After blooming is finished, it can be cut back by one-half or more to keep plants compact. Like arabis, aubretia dislikes standing water and it tends to melt out where night temperatures are warm. Do not cut plants back in the fall; wait until new growth shows in the spring. Plants tend to be short-lived.

PROPAGATION: By division, seed, or stem cuttings.

USES: Rockcress is a natural for rock gardens where it forms large carpets of bloom. They can also be planted in pockets of stone walls and do well in trough gardens. They are good for edging borders.

RELATED VARIETIES: 'Bengal Hybrids' produce larger-than-average flowers in rose, lilac, and deep red; 'Bressingham Red' has double red flowers; 'Carnival' produces a profusion of purple-violet flowers; and 'Purple Gem' bears purple flowers on 6-inch stems.

RUSSIAN SAGE
Perovskia species

Originally from Afghanistan and West Pakistan, Russian sage is beautiful and aromatic. It is a bushy perennial that is very drought tolerant and blooms for many weeks from midsummer through fall.

ZONE: USDA 5.

DESCRIPTION: Perovskia is a subshrub with a woody base. It produces gray-white stems up to 4 feet tall bearing finely textured, silvery, aromatic leaves. Large sprays of small ¼-inch, violet-blue flowers appear in late July and August. Flowers bloom from July through September. Both the foliage and the flowers are light and airy and bring a lacy texture to the garden.

EASY-CARE GROWING: Well-drained soil and a spot in full sun are the key requirements for these plants. Soil that stays wet in winter kills Russian sage. Space plants 3 feet apart to allow enough room for their full width at maturity. Plants sometimes flop over, especially when grown in rich soil. Try cutting plants back by one-half when they are 12 inches tall to produce fuller growth that is more likely to support upright stems. Russian sage grows easily and is not at all fussy—except in areas with a combination of high heat and humidity. Do not cut plants back in the fall; wait until new growth shows in the spring.

PROPAGATION: By cuttings.

USES: Planted in groups of three, as a hedge, or in a mass, these late-flowering plants will always elicit comments from garden visitors. Russian sage combines nicely with solidago, ornamental grasses, orange coneflower, and boltonia. The flowers are excellent when cut.

RELATED VARIETIES: 'Filigran' has filigreed foliage and blue flowers. 'Longin,' also sold as 'Blue Spires,' has deeply cut leaves and deep violet flower sprays.

SALVIA, MEADOW SAGE
Salvia x sylvestris (also S. nemerosa, S. x superba, and S. sylvestris var. superba)

When most people think of salvia they think of the annual variety, *Salvia splendens*, from Brazil, with blatant scarlet blossoms found in almost every public planting in America. But with over 700 species of salvia, there are many other hardy, half-hardy (USDA Zones 8 to 10), and annual salvias with better colors and greater charm available for gardens. With so many species, there is a great deal of confusion as to botanical names and classification, but you will find the plants described here sold as either *Salvia x sylvestris*, *S. nemerosa*, *S. x superba*, or *S. sylvestris* var. *superba*.

ZONE: USDA 4.

DESCRIPTION: Meadow sage has gray-green, paired leaves covered underneath with tiny hairs, on square stems. Some types grow up to 3 feet high while others stay around 15 inches tall. Plants bear many spikes of violet-purple or blue flowers in May and June that are attractive to butterflies and bees.

EASY-CARE GROWING: Salvia is easy to grow if given full sun and a good garden soil with excellent drainage. Remove faded flower spikes to encourage repeat bloom and cut leggy plants back to basal foliage if they become open in the center. Keep well watered until new growth begins.

PROPAGATION: By division or cuttings.

USES: Use salvias in drifts—the effect will be one of many flower spikes covered by pollinating insects. Many of the cultivars look great in combination with achillea. The combination of Salvia 'Blue Hills' or 'May Night' with yellow-flowered achillea is classic.

RELATED VARIETIES: 'Blue Hill' has true blue flowers and blooms for many weeks. 'Blue Queen' has deep violet flowers and good heat and drought tolerance. 'East Friesland' (or 'Oestfroesland') has 18-inch spikes of violet-blue flowers and grows well in hot climates. 'May Night' (or 'Mainacht') bears large indigo flowers with purple bracts on 18-inch stems.

SEDUM, STONECROP
Sedum species

There are perhaps 600 species of these succulent herbs—naturally occurring in the North Temperate Zone. Many make excellent garden subjects, but only a dozen species are usually found in nursery centers. Harder-to-find species can be located through various rock garden societies.

ZONE: USDA 4.

DESCRIPTION: With so many species, there is a great deal of variation in appearance and growth habit in this genus. In general though, sedums have strong stems with succulent, usually alternate leaves. Terminal clusters of small, star-shaped flowers have five petals.

EASY-CARE GROWING: Sedums need only a good, well-drained garden soil in full sun. They withstand drought and do amazingly well in very poor soils.

PROPAGATION: By seed, leaf cuttings, or division.

USES: The tall sedums, such as *Sedum spectabile*, are excellent in the bed and border, especially effective when planted in masses. The shorter, sprawling types are best for the rock garden. Some are good as ground covers. Most make excellent cut flowers.

RELATED SPECIES AND VARIETIES: *Sedum acre* grows in a 2- to 3-inch-tall carpet and bears yellow flowers in late spring. Plants grow easily in poor soil and can be used to fill difficult spots in full sun. *Sedum kamtschaticum* grows 4 to 9 inches tall and has deep green, scalloped leaves. It bears orange-yellow flowers from July to September. Grow on banks or slopes. *Sedum sieboldii* is a 4-inch-tall trailing plant with lightly scalloped blue-green leaves edged in pinkish-purple. Lovely pink flowers appear in late fall. *Sedum spurium* is a vigorous, mat-forming sedum that is evergreen through Zone 5. It sprouts showy red flowers in summer. Probably one of the top ten perennials in the garden world today is 'Autumn Joy.' Although best in full sun, plants will take light shade. They are always attractive: whether in tight buds of a light blue-green atop 2-foot stems; rosy pink in early bloom; in late bloom as the flowers turn mahogany; or a russet-brown during the winter. *S. spectabile* 'Brilliant' opens its flowers a month ahead of 'Autumn Joy.'

SNEEZEWEED, SWAMP SUNFLOWER
Helenium autumnale

There are many plants that begin blooming in early fall in bright colors that can often match those of autumn leaves. Sneezeweed is one such flower. Unfortunately, sneezeweed gets a bad rap for causing allergic reactions. However, it is not the culprit. Like goldenrod, it blooms at the same time as ragweed, which is the plant that sends people into spastic sneezing fits. It is a native American plant.

ZONE: USDA 3.

DESCRIPTION: Small daisies have downturned ray flowers on stout stems that branch toward the top and can reach 6 feet. Flowers are usually yellow or orange and plants bloom for a long time from late August through September. Sneezeweed grows 3 to 5 feet tall. Basal rosettes of leaves are evergreen in areas that have mild winters.

EASY-CARE GROWING: The plants are often found in dampish spots in the wild, and easily adapt to moist areas in the garden. During periods of drought, they need extra water. Grow in full sun. Plants should be pinched or cut back to keep them from getting too tall and leggy. If pinching, do so every other week from mid-May until mid-June. To cut back, remove one-half to two-thirds of the growth in early June.

PROPAGATION: By seed or division in spring.

USES: Sneezeweed provides beautiful color for the back of a border. It also stands out in an autumn or wild garden. Sneezeweed should be planted with ornamental grasses and fall asters. It is excellent for cutting.

RELATED VARIETIES: 'Butterpat' is 4 to 5 feet tall with yellow blooms; 'Coppelia' flowers earlier in the season with coppery-orange flowers on 3-foot stems; 'Crimson Beauty' grows 2 to 3 feet tall and has rich brown flowers; and 'Wyndley' is also 2 to 3 feet tall with coppery brown flowers.

Soapwort, Bouncing Bet

Saponaria officinalis

Soapwort was originally brought over to North America by colonists who used it as a soap substitute. This European immigrant has now naturalized over much of North America. When bruised or boiled in water, the leaves produce a lather that has detergent properties.

ZONE: USDA 2.

DESCRIPTION: Soapwort has stout, 12- to 24-inch stems, swollen at the joints, and oval, opposite leaves. It bears pink or white 1-inch flowers in clusters. The five united petals are especially fragrant at night.

EASY-CARE GROWING: Saponaria grows best in good, well-drained soil in full sun. Plants grown in overly rich soil tend to sprawl. Cut back in late spring after flowering to promote more compact growth and additional flowers. *Saponaria officinalis* is the most heat-tolerant species of the genus. It also blooms throughout the summer. Plants spread by way of underground stolons to form large colonies.

PROPAGATION: By division, cuttings, or seed.

USES: Saponaria is useful in the wild garden, in the bed or border, and even to carpet a slope or bank. Double-flowered forms are good cut flowers.

RELATED VARIETIES: 'Alba-plena' has double white flowers; 'Rosea-plena' has double rose-to-pink flowers; and 'Rubra Plena' is a form with double red flowers.

RELATED SPECIES: *Saponaria ocymoides*, or the rock soapwort, is a branching, trailing plant for the edge of the border or a rock wall, needing full sun and good drainage. Plants are usually 6 inches tall and covered in May and June with rose-pink flowers. They are prolific reseeders. 'Rubra compacta' has crimson flowers and is a nontrailing form, and 'Splendens' bears deep rose-pink blossoms on 4-inch plants. *S. x lempergii* 'Max Frei' has loads of large pink flowers but does not tolerate heat or poorly drained soil. Grow in a rock garden or raised bed where water moves out of the soil quickly.

Fragrant Solomon's Seal

Polygonatum odoratum

Solomon's seal is a graceful native woodland plant that slowly forms large colonies. The variegated form stands out from a distance and is much used by landscape architects.

Zone: USDA 3.

Description: Solomon's seal is distinguished by its 18- to 24-inch-tall arching stems with alternate green leaves. Pendulous, white or creamy, bell-shaped flowers burst forth in spring. They hang down underneath the leaves and are subtly fragrant. The flowers are followed by 1-inch-diameter blue-black fruit in the summer.

Easy-care growing: Solomon's seal grows well in heavy or moderate shade in moist soil that is rich in organic matter. Keep soil moist by watering during dry periods in summer. Plants purchased at garden centers will probably look rather forlorn with a single, weak-looking stem arising from a large pot. Don't let this put you off—buy it anyway and keep the soil around new plantings moist. Solomon's seal takes two years to get established, then it spreads readily by underground rhizomes. Be careful not to cultivate around the shallow-rooted plants because you can damage rhizomes that creep along—or just below—the surface of the soil.

Propagation: By division in fall.

Uses: Naturalize in a woodland garden, or plant under shrubs and small trees. Solomon's seal mixes well with hosta, astilbe, and ferns but you may have to remove some of the plants occasionally to keep them from crowding neighbors. The foliage is excellent in flower arrangements.

Related variety: 'Variegatum' is the most attractive and most common variety. Soft green leaves have wide margins of creamy white. The variegation really brightens dark shade gardens.

SPEEDWELL, SPIKED SPEEDWELL
Veronica spicata

The genus Veronica contains at least ten garden-worthy species but *V. spicata* is the most commonly planted. These strong growers provide good color in perennial gardens for many weeks.

ZONE: USDA 3.

DESCRIPTION: Plants have simple, oblong, 2-inch-long glossy leaves. Stems grow 10 to 36 inches tall, depending on the variety. The stems of taller types often bend over and then turn upward. Stems end in densely branched spikes of small blue, pink, or white flowers that bloom for four to seven weeks in summer.

EASY-CARE GROWING: Speedwell succeeds in any good, well-drained garden soil in full sun. Be sure to deadhead for repeat bloom. Wet winter soil is usually fatal to speedwell.

PROPAGATION: By division or stem cuttings.

USES: The taller varieties are beautiful in the middle of the garden and shorter varieties are good at the front. They also make good cut flowers.

RELATED VARIETIES: 'Blue Peter' bears deep blue flowers in July and August on 24-inch stems; 'Icicle' is pure white on 18-inch plants and blooms from June to September; 'Red Fox' blooms with deep rose-red flowers on 14-inch stems; 'Sunny Border Blue' has violet-blue spikes that bloom from June until hard frost; and 'Waterperry' grows 6 inches tall and bears an abundance of light blue flowers in spring.

RELATED SPECIES AND VARIETIES: *Veronica alpina* 'Goodness Grows' stands 12 inches tall and sports long blue flower spikes for many weeks. *Veronica austriaca* (syn. *latifolia*) 'Crater Lake Blue' is an excellent front-of-the-border plant bearing deep gentian-blue flowers on 15-inch stems. *Veronica prostrata* is a mat-forming type with deep blue flowers on 4-inch stems. 'Heavenly Blue' has sapphire blue flowers.

SPIDERWORT
Tradescantia virginiana (syn. x *andersoniana*)

Spiderworts are like daylilies—each blossom lasts only one day. However, flowers open over a period of six to eight weeks providing a good show of color for almost two months.

ZONE: USDA 4.

DESCRIPTION: The Spiderwort is a weak-stemmed plant that grows 1 to 2 feet tall. It produces a watery juice in the folded, strap-like leaves. The three-petaled flowers, opening at dawn and fading by mid-afternoon, are surrounded by many new flower buds. Flowers are purple, white, pink, or red.

EASY-CARE GROWING: Spiderwort grows best in good, well-drained, moist garden soil in full sun or partial shade. They grow well in wet soil but will tolerate drier conditions. If soil is overly rich, they grow quickly and tumble about. Most plants turn brown after they flower or the leaves become marred by a fungal disease called rust. If either occurs, cut plants back to the ground and keep them well watered until new growth starts. It is possible that you will get a light rebloom. Divide plants every three years to keep them vigorous and to control spread.

PROPAGATION: By division in spring.

USES: Although fine in the sunny border, spiderwort grows best in areas of open shade—especially under tall trees. They can be planted in low-lying areas with moist soil or near the edges of ponds and streams.

RELATED VARIETIES: 'Isis' has 3-inch light blue flowers; 'J.C. Weguelin' has 2½-inch-wide China blue flowers; 'Red Cloud' has deep-rose-red flowers; 'Snow Cap' is pure white; and 'Zwanenberg' has very large, blue flowers. All grow to a height of about 20 inches.

SPOTTED NETTLE, DEAD NETTLE
Lamium maculatum

The nettles are generally weedy plants. However, one or two species are valued for the garden. The appellation "dead" serves to differentiate this plant from stinging nettle (*Utrica dioica*).

ZONE: USDA 3.

DESCRIPTION: Dead nettles are sprawling plants with square stems, toothed oval leaves, and 1-inch-long flowers that resemble small snapdragons. Purplish-red flowers appear in May and June and continue blooming sporadically through summer. Leaves usually have white or silver markings. Spotted nettle grows 8 to 12 inches tall and 18 inches wide.

EASY-CARE GROWING: Lamiums are not fussy, doing well in a good, well-drained garden soil in partial shade. They are more robust in moist soil, but tolerate occasional drought. However, if the soil dries out too often, bare patches develop. If foliage deteriorates in the heat of summer, cut plants back to basal foliage and keep well watered. The new growth will soon appear.

PROPAGATION: By division in spring.

USES: Lamiums are excellent ground covers for small areas and border edgings in formal, wild, or woodland gardens. Their variegated leaves are as attractive as the flowers.

RELATED VARIETIES: 'Beacon Silver' has silver leaves with dark green edges and pink flowers; 'Pink Pewter' has pink flowers and silver leaves with green margins; 'White Nancy' is a white-flowered form.

RELATED SPECIES: *Lamium galeobdolon*, yellow archangel, spreads by underground stolons and is an aggressive ground cover that works well when planted in dense shade under shrubs or trees. It should not be mixed with other perennials. Small yellow flowers appear in spring. Leaves are 1 to 3 inches long and oval. Cut plants back when they become leggy. 'Herman's Pride' is a more compact variety with smaller leaves and flowers. The foliage has handsome silver markings. It can be mixed with other perennials such as hosta, ferns, and brunnera. 'Variegatum' is the common form with silver variegation.

CUSHION SPURGE
Euphorbia epithymoides (syn. *polychroma*)

These plants are in the same genus as the familiar Christmas poinsettia. Both have very small flowers and what we perceive to be petals are really colored leaves called bracts. Poinsettia bracts are red, white, or pink; spurge bracts are bright yellow or chartreuse. When cut, the stems of all euphorbias release a milky latex sap.

ZONE: USDA 5.

DESCRIPTION: Cushion spurge has oblong, light green leaves that grow in a clump 12 to 14 inches high and 14 inches wide. Plants are covered with yellow to chartreuse bracts in spring—the color itself looks as though it were applied with an artist's airbrush. The leaves turn red in the fall.

EASY-CARE GROWING: Cushion spurge prefers a good, well-drained garden soil. It will grow in full sun in Zones 4 and 5 but appreciates afternoon shade. In warmer regions, plant in partial shade. Plants grown in southern regions tend to get floppy after a few years. To avoid this, divide every two or three years and replace old plantings with the new divisions or with new cutting-propagated plants.

PROPAGATION: By division, seed, or stem cuttings after plants flower.

USES: Cushion spurge looks good in front of a low wall or grouped on a low bank. It also works well at the edge of a lightly shaded garden.

RELATED VARIETY: 'Purpurea' has purplish leaves that contrast well with the flowers.

RELATED SPECIES: *Euphorbia amygdaloides*, wood spurge, is hardy to Zone 5. It prefers moist soil and cool climates and grows in upright mounds. The stems are purple and the flower bracts are chartreuse. Plants are evergreen and flowers are produced on the previous season's growth. 'Purpurea' (syn. 'Rubra') has deep red stems and bronze leaves. Robb's spurge, *E. amygdaloides* var. *robbiae*, has green leaves and chartreuse bracts.

STOKE'S ASTER
Stokesia laevis

Stoke's aster is a native American originally found from South Carolina to Florida and Louisiana. It is surprisingly hardy as far north as Rochester, New York. Intensive breeding has resulted in large, colorful flowers that are great both in the garden and in flower arrangements.

ZONE: USDA 5.

DESCRIPTION: Leaves are alternate, about 6 inches long, and have a distinctive white midrib. Basal leaves remain evergreen through the winter. Fluffy blue to lavender flowers are 2 to 5 inches across on well-branched, 1- to 2-foot stems.

EASY-CARE GROWING: Stokesia needs filtered sun and a good, well-drained soil. New plants take a year or two to settle in before maximum bloom. They should be mulched in areas with severe winters and little snow cover. Flowers bloom for about four weeks but blooming can be extended by regular deadheading. Several flowers are borne on a single stem but only one opens at a time. To remove old flowers, inspect old and new buds carefully because old buds look similar to new ones after the petals fall off. Plants are drought tolerant after they are established. Divide plants every four years to keep them at peak bloom.

PROPAGATION: By division in spring.

USES: Stokesia has very decorative flowers that should be featured at the front of the bed or border. They are good cut flowers, lasting for a week in fresh arrangements, and the seedpods are excellent in dried arrangements.

RELATED VARIETIES: 'Alba' is a pure white form; 'Blue Danube' is lavender-blue; 'Mary Gregory' has unusual yellow flowers; and 'Silver Moon' has creamy white flowers.

ORNAMENTAL STRAWBERRY, ALPINE STRAWBERRY

Fragaria species

Increasing numbers of beautiful, edible plants are finding their way into perennial gardens. Among these are bronze fennel, ornamental sweet potato vine, rhubarb, and ornamental strawberry. Ornamental strawberry is a great ground cover that quickly fills large areas.

ZONE: USDA 3.

DESCRIPTION: Plants grow about 6 inches tall. Mother plants spread quickly by runners that end in new plants. Ornamental strawberries produce small fruit but not in great numbers.

EASY-CARE GROWING: Plant in full sun or light shade in soil with good drainage. Excessive moisture causes plants to rot. Don't let plants dry out in summer or the leaves will turn brown and brittle. Plants are usually semi-evergreen so winter-damaged foliage needs to be cleaned up in the spring. Do not prune or clean up in the fall.

USES: Ornamental strawberry can be used as a ground cover and in hanging baskets and containers. It is too aggressive to mix with other perennials but makes a fine ground cover when planted by itself.

RELATED VARIETIES: 'Lipstick' has flowers that are rose-red. It blooms heavily in spring then intermittently throughout summer. Foliage is light green. 'Pink Panda' has large pink flowers that bloom from spring through frost. The leaves are dark green and glossy.

RELATED SPECIES: *Fragaria vesca* 'Improved Rugen' is a very hardy plant that does not produce runners, so it can be used to edge walkways and garden beds. Flowers are white and produce juicy, sweet fruit from June through October. 'Vesca' is especially prolific late in the season.

SUNDROP, EVENING PRIMROSE
Oenothera species

The day-bloomers in this genus are the sundrops, and the common name is a perfect choice for petals that look like molten gold. The night-bloomers are called evening primrose. They are often found in mature, old-fashioned gardens. Many are natives of the United States.

ZONES: USDA 4 and 5.

DESCRIPTION: Sundrops have simple, alternate leaves on strong stems that grow up to 2 feet high. They are topped by clusters of bright yellow, four-petaled flowers up to 2 inches across, that bloom in the summer. Some *Oenothera* species have white or pink flowers. Flowers open for only a day or two but many buds are produced, resulting in a long flowering period. Basal rosettes are evergreen in colder areas.

EASY-CARE GROWING: Sundrops and evening primrose are extremely tolerant of poor soil and are very drought resistant, but the ground must be well drained and full sun is necessary. If given a spot in good soil, they become quite pushy, but are easily controlled by digging since they are shallow-rooted.

PROPAGATION: By seed or division in spring.

USES: Sundrops are perfect for the wild garden and can hold their own at the edge of a field or meadow. Most of the flowers can be gathered for winter bouquets because the seedpods are very attractive.

RELATED SPECIES: There are a number of species useful for the garden. *Oenothera fruticosa*, common sundrop, is an upright wildflower of the eastern United States with 2-inch yellow flowers on 1½- to 2-foot reddish stems and is the type usually found in old gardens. *Oenothera missourensis* creeps along the ground and grows about 1 foot high. The showy blossoms are paper thin and 4 inches wide. The trailing stems carry a succession of lemon-yellow flowers opening in early afternoon. Sharp drainage is essential for good growth. The seedpods are very attractive. *Oenothera berlandieri* (syn. *O. speciosa*) has slender, creeping stems that grow 6 to 12 inches tall and bear 1-inch rose-pink flowers. 'Siskiyou' produces 2-inch pink flowers on 8-inch-tall plants.

MANY-FLOWERED SUNFLOWER
Helianthus x *multiflorus*

Perennial sunflowers are very valuable for their late-season bloom, and their bright yellow flowers combine well with asters, boltonia, and ornamental grasses in September.

ZONE: USDA 4.

DESCRIPTION: Perennial sunflowers are tall—3 to 5 feet—robust plants with fibrous roots and large, rough, simple leaves on stout stems. Large, yellow, daisylike flowers bloom in September and October for four to six weeks.

EASY-CARE GROWING: Grow many-flowered sunflower in full sun and good, moist garden soil. Provide supplemental water during periods of drought. Foliage usually looks pretty ragged after flowering, so cut back after the flowers are spent.

PROPAGATION: By seed or division after flowering.

USES: Perennial sunflowers are best grown in the back of the border or in the wild garden. They are excellent cut flowers and, if old flowers are left in place, birds will feast on the seeds.

RELATED VARIETY: 'Flore Pleno' is the most common cultivar. It sports double blossoms that look more like chrysanthemums than sunflowers. 'Morning Sun' has single, yellow flowers with brown centers and grows 5 feet tall.

RELATED SPECIES: *Helianthus angustifolius*, or the swamp sunflower, is native from New York to Florida and west to Texas where it grows in wet or boggy areas. If moved to good garden soil and provided with extra water during periods of drought, the 6-foot plants will bloom in September with 3-inch-wide, yellow daisies. However, it is only hardy to Zone 6. *Helianthus salicifolius*, or willow-leaved sunflower, is an American native from the Midwest. Although the 2-inch-wide sunflowers are pretty when blooming in the fall, this plant is used for its attractive willowlike foliage. Plants reach about 4 feet in height and grow easily in well-drained, alkaline garden soil. Plants can self-seed prolifically so you will probably want to remove unwanted seedlings.

SUNFLOWER HELIOPSIS, FALSE SUNFLOWER
Heliopsis helianthoides

Ox-eyes are native American plants found from New York to Michigan and south to Georgia. Members of the daisy family, they are similar to true sunflowers (Helianthus) but Heliopsis blooms earlier in the season and is shorter.

ZONE: USDA 3.

DESCRIPTION: Heliopsis sports yellow or orange daisies, often 3 inches in diameter, on stout stems that grow between 3 and 5 feet tall. The leaves are simple and toothed. Flowers bloom from summer to frost.

EASY-CARE GROWING: These plants will bloom the first year from seed. Although they want full sun, ox-eyes will tolerate partial shade. They need a good, well-drained garden soil and require extra water during periods of drought. Plants are moderate self-seeders and unwanted seedlings are easily removed by hoeing. Plants grown in rich soil may need to be divided every three years or so to increase vigor. Plants grown in less fertile soil probably won't need division until they've been in the ground five years.

PROPAGATION: By seed or division in spring.

USES: Since their cheerful flowers bloom over such a long period, ox-eyes are valuable in a bed, a border, or in a wild garden. The flowers are excellent for cutting.

RELATED VARIETIES: 'Ballerina' (syn. 'Ballet Dancer') is 3 feet tall with bright yellow semi-double flowers. 'Gold Greenheart' has double, yellow-green flowers with a green center when newly opened. 'Golden Plume' is a good double-flowered variety with yellow blooms about 2½ inches across.

RELATED SPECIES: *Heliopsis helianthoides* 'Summer Sun' has soft yellow flowers and grows 3 feet tall.

THYME
Thymus species

Thyme is usually relegated to the herb garden but its low-growing, creeping habit makes it a natural for edging and planting in between stepping stones in a sunny perennial garden. There are hundreds of species—some are best left to culinary use because they get tall and rangy, and others are compact and good in ornamental gardens. It is important to get the right species for use in a perennial garden.

ZONE: USDA 5.

DESCRIPTION: Stems are either trailing or upright with small, elliptic leaves that are very fragrant. Many species are evergreen. Pink or lavender flowers occur on short, dense spikes. The flowers are very attractive to honeybees.

EASY-CARE GROWING: All species need full sun and good drainage. Plants will rot in soil that stays wet for long periods. Thyme grows very well all summer in northern gardens where the climate is not as hot and humid as in the South. If plants melt out due to high heat and humidity, cut them back and new growth will emerge. Plants will be fuller and more vigorous if they are pruned back frequently up until August. (Pruning after this may result in tissue that is not hardy enough to survive the first hard freeze.) Do not cut plants back during fall or winter garden cleanup—wait until new growth emerges in spring.

PROPAGATION: By seed, division, or stem cuttings.

USES: Perennial thyme can be used as an edging plant, between stepping stones, in pockets in stone walls, and in containers.

RELATED SPECIES AND VARIETIES: *Thymus* x *citriodorus*, lemon thyme, smells like lemons and grows 9 to 12 inches tall. Look for the pretty variegated forms. *T. herbabarona*, caraway thyme, smells like caraway and is a robust plant that grows 2 to 5 inches tall. *Thymus praecox*, mother-of-thyme, is the traditional dark green ground cover that grows 4 inches tall. *T. pseudolanuginosus*, woolly thyme, has minute, woolly silver leaves and stays low to the ground. *T. serphyllum*, wild thyme, grows 4 to 6 inches tall and is used extensively as a ground cover. 'Coccineus' bears tiny rose-colored flowers and forms a dense mat.

TOAD LILY
Tricyrtis hirta

It's unfortunate that such an attractive and unusual flower should have a swampy name like "toad lily." Rumor has it that the juice of these plants is used by indigenous people when hunting frogs. It is rubbed on one's hands in preparation for the hunt because it is attractive to frogs and makes them less slippery. True or not, it's a charming story.

ZONE: USDA 4.

DESCRIPTION: Plants have alternate, 6-inch leaves on arching, hairy stems that are usually 2 to 3 feet high. They bear creamy white flower buds, often in clusters, which open to funnel-shaped flowers with white petals and purple spots. Flowers are about 1 inch across, blooming in late August or September and continuing for several weeks. Plants form 2- to 3-foot clumps.

EASY-CARE GROWING: Toad lilies need moist, fertile soil with a high humus content and partial shade—or the open shade found beneath trees. Toad lily is long-lived but if division is necessary, do it in early spring while plants are dormant.

PROPAGATION: By seed or division in spring.

USES: Toad lilies should be planted where they are easily seen. The plants are especially valuable for the shade garden because they are among the few that bloom so late in the garden year. Toad lily can be used in woodland gardens or in more formal shade gardens.

RELATED VARIETIES: 'Miyazaki' has pink to white flowers with crimson spots. 'Variegata' has lavender flowers and leaves that are narrowly edged in gold.

RELATED SPECIES: *Tricyrtis formosana* is a stoloniferous type that grows 1 to 2 feet tall and spreads to form good-sized clumps. The flowers are spotted with crimson, face upward, and are star-shaped.

VERBENA
Verbena species

A multitude of tender verbenas have been used in annual gardens over the years, but now there are several good perennial species that are hardy in the warmer zones.

ZONES: USDA 6, 7, and 8.

DESCRIPTION: Verbena blooms for a long time, and all perennial species have small purple flowers borne in flat, terminal clumps. The flowers attract butterflies, bees, and other pollinating insects throughout the growing season. Stems are usually four-sided. Height and growth habit vary according to the species.

EASY-CARE GROWING: Full sun and well-drained soil on the lean side suit perennial verbena. Flowers should be deadheaded after they fade to maximize repeat bloom.

PROPAGATION: By seed, stem cuttings, and root cuttings.

USES: Use in the perennial garden depends on the species.

RELATED SPECIES AND VARIETIES: *Verbena bonariensis*, Brazilian verbena, grows 3 to 4 feet tall and has a very airy texture. It works well when used in groups of three or more as a filler plant or in a larger mass in the middle of a perennial garden. The lilac flowers start opening in May and continue until frost. It is hardy to USDA Zone 6 and often comes back from self-sown seedlings in Zone 5. *V. canadensis*, rose verbena, is much shorter in stature at 8 to 12 inches tall. Trailing stems stay close to the ground and end in heads of rose-red flowers. Plants root where the stems touch the ground and spread rapidly—but they can be easily cut back. 'Homestead Purple' bears dark purple flowers and is quite vigorous. Rose verbena is hardy to Zone 8. *V. rigida*, rigid verbena, grows 12 to 24 inches tall and is hardy to Zone 7. It is very heat- and drought-tolerant and looks like a shorter version of Brazilian verbena.

VIRGINIA BLUEBELLS
Mertensia virginica

Virginia bluebells are a delightful spring wildflower with soft, cool green foliage and two-toned pink and blue flowers. They make a beautiful carpet under deciduous trees and are the perfect foil for daffodils. Because bluebells go dormant and disappear after flowering they are referred to as "spring ephemerals."

ZONE: USDA 3.

DESCRIPTION: Virginia bluebells grow 2 feet tall and form dense colonies in wooded areas in early spring. Loads of two-toned bell-shaped flowers hang down from the stems in large clusters. Flower buds are pink and turn lavender-blue as they age. Plants spread by seedlings and, over time, will colonize a large area that is to their liking. Foliage yellows and disappears after plants quit flowering.

EASY-CARE GROWING: Plant where soil is rich in organic matter and moist. Plants will tolerate sun in cooler climates but grow best under deciduous trees where they get sun in spring and are shaded through the summer.

PROPAGATION: By division of mature plantings in the spring or seed (it must be fresh).

USES: Naturalize in wooded areas or mix with hosta and ferns, which will cover bare spots left by dormant bluebells.

WORMWOOD
Artemisia species

With the exception of *Artemisia lactiflora*, or mugwort, wormwoods are grown for their handsome silver foliage. The flowers are not very desirable and are often removed before they open.

ZONE: USDA 3.

DESCRIPTION: Wormwoods are shrublike plants that usually have attractive, silver-gray foliage and sprays of small, mostly unattractive flowers. The leaves and other plant parts are often aromatic.

EASY-CARE GROWING: Plants prefer poor, sandy soil over deep, fertile earth. They must have full sun and good drainage or the roots will soon rot. Keep plants pruned and shaped through the spring and summer so they don't get leggy or open up in the center. Do not bother growing in areas with high summer humidity and lots of rain. Refrain from cutting back in the fall and winter. Wait until new growth appears in the spring before tidying up.

PROPAGATION: By division or seed.

USES: The larger plants can be used as backgrounds to borders; individual plants enhance colorful blossoms—especially white, pink, or lavender flowers. Dried specimens are excellent in winter bouquets.

RELATED SPECIES: *Artemisia arbotanum*, or southernwood, can be used as a deciduous hedge as it can grow to a height of 4 feet. The leaves are spicy smelling, bright green, and fernlike. *A. absinthium*, or common wormwood, has shiny silver, finely cut foliage on 3-foot stems. 'Lambrook Silver' has very finely textured leaves and is more gray-green than the species. *A. lactiflora*, or white mugwort, is the only one of this group grown for the flowers, which are not really white but more of a cream color. Masses of these tiny blossoms crowd 5-foot stems, starting in late summer and on into autumn. This plant needs better soil than the others. *A. schmidtiana* 'Silver Mound' grows in rounded balls with feathery, cut foliage to about 20 inches wide. *A. stelleriana*, or beach wormwood, is the only member of the genus to grow well in humid regions and is often found naturalized along sandy beaches of the Northeast. Plants grow about 2½ feet high.

YARROW
Achillea species

Most people have seen the wild form of yarrow, *Achillea millefolium*, a wildflower originally from Europe and western Asia. It has whitish or deep pink flowers and is often used—along with bachelor's buttons—in highway medians and other municipal plantings.

ZONE: USDA 3.

DESCRIPTION: Yarrow grows between 1 and 3 feet high, blooming from June until August—and sometimes until frost. Flowers are small and arranged in large flat heads on top of stout stems. The foliage is finely cut and resembles that of a fern. Most species are aromatic and smell of chamomile. Yarrows with silvery-gray leaves are clump-forming plants that do not spread much while those with green leaves spread rapidly to form a solid mat of foliage.

EASY-CARE GROWING: Yarrows are especially valuable as they are tolerant of drought and suitable for any reasonably fertile garden soil that has good drainage. Plants will rot if the soil stays too wet. They revel in full sun and should be deadheaded to prolong bloom. Some of the taller types, such as 'Coronation Gold,' may need staking. If flowering diminishes after two or three years, divide plants and replant small, non-woody divisions to get them going again.

PROPAGATION: By division in spring or fall.

USES: Yarrow is especially suitable for the garden border and looks good in masses. It is excellent both for fresh cut flowers and dried for winter bouquets.

RELATED VARIETIES AND SPECIES: *Achillea* x 'Anthea' has gray-green foliage that does not spread. Sulfur-yellow flower heads are 2 to 3 inches across and do not need staking. Plants grow 1 to 2 feet tall and 1 foot wide. *Achillea* x 'Coronation Gold' bears large heads of golden-yellow flowers and is excellent for drying. Plants grow 2 to 4 feet tall and 3 feet wide. The wildflower, *Achillea millefolium*, is suited for the meadow or wild garden. It spreads aggressively. *Achillea* x 'Moonshine' has bright yellow flowers on 2-foot stems.

INDEX

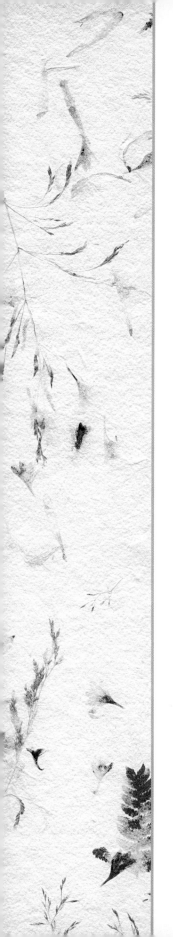

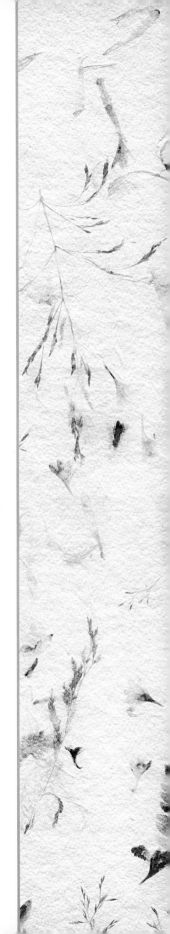